Memories of 'Abdu'l-Bahá

Memories of 'Abdu'l-Bahá

Recollections
of the
Early Days of the
Bahá'í Faith in California

Ramona Allen Brown

Bahá'í Publishing Trust
Wilmette, Illinois 60091

Copyright © 1980 by the
National Spiritual Assembly of the
Bahá'ís of the United States

World Rights Reserved

Library of Congress Cataloging in Publication Data

Brown, Ramona Allen, 1889–1975.
   Memories of 'Abdu'l-Bahá.

   Includes bibliographical references and index.
   1. Brown, Ramona Allen, 1889–1975. 2. Bahaism—California. 3. 'Abd ul-Bahá ibn Bahá Ulláh, 1884–1921. 4. Bahaism—Biography. I. Title.
BP395.B76A35   297'.89'0924   79–16412
ISBN 0-87743-128-0

Designed by John Solarz

Printed in the United States of America

10 9 8 7 6 5 4 3 2 1

This book is lovingly dedicated
to my daughter, Barbara Bray West,
and my son, J. Allen Bray.

Contents

Illustrations ix
Foreword xv
Preface xix
Acknowledgment xxiii
Part 1: Early Believers in California 1
Part 2: 'Abdu'l-Bahá in California 31
Part 3: After 'Abdu'l-Bahá Returned to Haifa 89
Part 4: Coda 109
Notes 123
Index 135

Illustrations

Plate

I HELEN GOODALL   between
called by 'Abdu'l-Bahá the   pp. 8–9
"Spiritual Mother of the [Oakland]
Confirmed Community," standing
in the garden of the Master's home
in Haifa in 1920.

II Home of Helen Goodall at 1537
Jackson Street, Oakland, California,
where Bahá'í meetings were held
around 1900.

III ELLA GOODALL COOPER
addressed by 'Abdu'l-Bahá as
"Jewel of the Spirit" and termed by
Shoghi Effendi a herald of the
Covenant and a "dearly loved
handmaid" of 'Abdu'l-Bahá.

IV FRANCES ORR ALLEN and
DR. WOODSON ALLEN
at whose home were held the first
Bahá'í meetings in Berkeley,
California.

V LUA GETSINGER
named by 'Abdu'l-Bahá a "Herald
of the Covenant" and by Shoghi
Effendi the "Mother Teacher of the
West."

VI PHOEBE APPERSON HEARST
called by 'Abdu'l-Bahá the "Mother
of the Faithful."

VII MAY BOLLES (MAXWELL) and
     AGNES ALEXANDER
       shown together in Portland,
       Oregon, in 1924.
VIII THORNTON CHASE   *between*
       designated by 'Abdu'l-Bahá as the   pp. 24–25
       first American Bahá'í.
IX   THE HACIENDA
       a photograph of Phoebe Hearst's
       Hacienda at Pleasanton, California,
       taken about the time 'Abdu'l-Bahá
       visited there in 1912.
X   Views of the entrance of the
       Hacienda, home of Phoebe Hearst
       at Pleasanton, California, showing
       the station of the gatekeeper at the
       right and the entrance through
       which 'Abdu'l-Bahá walked during
       His visit of October 13–16, 1912.
XI   LUA GETSINGER and GEORGIA
     RALSTON
XII SOME OF THE "PEACH TREE"
       Front row, left to right: Ramona
         Allen (Bray Brown), Marie Barr
         (Bray), Betty Vent (Smith), and
         Ethel Sternberg.
       Back row, left to right: Edith
         Woodward (Loomis), Eva
         Benjamin (?), Cicely Alderman
         (Potter), and Helen Barr (Tice).
XIII ELLA BAILEY
       (right) shown (right to left) with
       ROBERT GULICK, MADAM
       FARAJU'LLAH (mother of Bahia
       Gulick), and RAMONA BROWN in
       Berkeley, California, May 7, 1950.
XIV 'ABDU'L-BAHÁ   *between*
       standing in the quadrangle in front pp. 41–42
       of the Memorial Chapel of Leland
       Stanford Junior University, Palo

	Alto, California, where He spoke on October 8, 1912.	
XV	'ABDU'L-BAHÁ shown surrounded by children and their parents on the steps of the home of Helen Goodall in Oakland, California, after His meeting with the children on October 12, 1912.	
XVI	THE ALLEN FAMILY Back row, left to right: Frances Orr Allen, Dr. Woodson Allen. Front row, left to right: Ramona Allen, Joseph Bray, Gertrude Mitchell (Allen), Warren Allen.	
XVII	Lloyd Lake in Golden Gate Park in San Francisco where 'Abdu'l-Bahá would leave the automobile and walk along the shore, then stand and watch the ducks swim toward Him. In the background is the marble arch, called "Portals of the Past," from the Towne family mansion. The author is shown visiting the spot in 1965.	
XVIII	'ABDU'L-BAHÁ with friends from many cities, including some of the "Peach Tree," gathered for the Feast on October 16, 1912, at the home of Helen Goodall in Oakland, California.	*between* pp. 72–73
XIX	Views of the balcony and stained glass window in the home of Helen Goodall in Oakland, California, where 'Abdu'l-Bahá stood and chanted a benediction after the Feast on October 16, 1912.	
XX	'ABDU'L-BAHÁ walking in front of the home of Helen Goodall in Oakland,	

XXI	California, on October 23, 1912. 'ABDU'L-BAHÁ in front of the Goodall home on October 23, 1912, talking with friends, including a group of East Indian students who had attended Frances Orr Allen's Bahá'í classes in Berkeley.	
XXII	MARTHA ROOT Hand of the Cause of God and called by Shoghi Effendi the "Leading Ambassadress of His Faith."	*between* pp. 104–105
XXIII	JOHN and LOUISE BOSCH gave land for the site of the Bahá'í school at Geyserville, California.	
XXIV	MARK TOBEY and KATHRYN FRANKLAND at a Bahá'í convention in Wilmette, Illinois. BAHÁ' Í CHILDREN'S CLASS taught by Kathryn Frankland in Berkeley, California, in the early days. Front row, left to right: Nephew of Ella Cooper (holding child), unknown, niece of Ella Cooper, and Barbara Bray. Back row, left to right: Niece of Ella Cooper (in hat), niece of Ella Cooper, Helen Frankland (with hairbow, daughter of Kathryn), niece of Ella Cooper, (child) Allen Bray, and Lorne Mattesen.	
XXV	'ABDU'L-BAHÁ and friends, including the pilgrims from California in 1920, shown in front of the Shrine of the Báb on Mt. Carmel.	

Front row, seated, left to right of 'Abdu'l-Bahá: Emogene Hoagg, Georgia Ralston, Helen Goodall, Julie Culver, Ella Cooper, and Kathryn Frankland.
Back row: Saichiro Fujita (back of Ella Cooper).

Foreword

On February 23, 1975, at the age of eighty-six, Ramona Allen Brown passed from this world, in La Jolla, California, concluding a long and fruitful life of service to the Cause of Bahá'u'lláh. It was a life that spanned the twenty-nine years during which 'Abdu'l-Bahá guided the Bahá'í Faith and the thirty-six years of Shoghi Effendi's Guardianship and that saw, in 1963, the election of the first Universal House of Justice. Ramona was born in Boulder Creek, California, in 1889, the only daughter of Dr. Woodson and Frances Orr Allen. She became a Bahá'í in Oakland in 1904 at the age of fifteen while visiting Helen Goodall, the "spiritual mother" of the Oakland community. To her parents' home came many of the early Bahá'í teachers in America: Lua Getsinger, Thornton Chase, Isabella Brittingham, Helen Goodall, Ella Cooper, Ali-Kuli Khan, Martha Root, Clara and Hyde Dunn. As Ramona grew to womanhood, she counted these and many other distinguished Bahá'ís—Phoebe Hearst, Kanichi Yamamoto, Emogene Hoagg, Georgia Ralston, Saichiro Fujita, Ella Bailey, Agnes Alexander, John and Louise Bosch, Kathryn Frankland, John and Annie Linfoot and their daughters Gladys and Charlotte—among her friends. Ramona was among that stalwart band of Bahá'ís who welcomed 'Abdu'l-Bahá to California in 1912.

Ramona Allen Brown lived for many years in California, raising her family, teaching the Bahá'í Faith, and helping to consolidate the growing Bahá'í community. In 1954, at the age of sixty-five, she made a pilgrimage to the World Center of the Bahá'í Faith in Haifa, Israel. Afterward came a new chapter in her service to the Cause. Though she had never been physically strong, Shoghi Effendi, the Guardian of the Bahá'í Faith, suggested that she visit Bahá'í teachers in the Mediterranean islands. This she did, then she settled in Majorca and later in Austria, where she remained for seven years. In Salzburg she served on the first Local Spiritual Assembly, and she brought into the Bahá'í Faith the first native Austrian believer.

In December 1963, at her doctor's insistence, Mrs. Brown returned to California for a few months' respite from the rigorous Austrian winter, planning to resume her post in the spring. But that was not to be. At the request of Dr. Ugo Giachery, she stayed in San Diego with his ailing wife while he was on a teaching trip in Central America, then remained in La Jolla in her beloved California until her death. As in the early days, before and after 'Abdu'l-Bahá's visit, she continued to teach the Faith. She was particularly fond of retelling the stories of 'Abdu'l-Bahá's momentous visit to California, drawing youth and adults alike to hear the accounts of the precious days the Master had spent in the state He likened to the Holy Land. Indeed, during the last few years of her life, even though suffering from poor health, Mrs. Brown never taught more actively: the youth would bring lunch to her hotel and stay all day, listening to her speak about Bahá'í administration, the Covenant, and the visit of 'Abdu'l-Bahá. While completing her book during this same period, she wrote that "it has been a source of great joy and bounty to have been able to share my memories and experience in the Faith with the Bahá'ís around the world over a period of years. Now it is my hope that many others will find it possible to read about them in my book and gain both pleasure and insight from what I have been able to write down about those wonderful and historic times."

Editing someone's memories when he is alive is a challenge. Editing those same memories after he is dead is an even greater challenge, particularly when one knows that they were "written from the heart" and that the author was very particular about saying things as she would say them. Such was the task facing us with Ramona Brown's recollections of 'Abdu'l-Bahá and the early days of the Faith in California. Our editing has been extremely light. When absolutely necessary, we added transitional words, phrases, and sentences to keep the reader from being cast adrift. For the same reason we moved entire passages to conclude a story, enhance a theme, or bring out the inherent structure. But we always looked to Mrs. Brown for clues on wording and style.

Documentation of all details in the memoirs proved even more difficult. We verified the published sources and as many of the unpublished sources as possible, indicating differences in the notes. The many quoted passages that are not footnoted come either from Mrs. Brown's recollections or from sources the editors were not able to find and check. In such passages the editors used the house style of punctuation and of the transliteration of Persian and Arabic words.

The variety of the sources used in the book, ranging as they do from authorized, published translations of the works of Bahá'u'lláh, 'Abdu'l-Bahá, and Shoghi Effendi, to unpublished translations of Tablets of 'Abdu'l-Bahá sent to the early Bahá'ís, to stenographically recorded talks, informal notes, letters, and memories of numerous events, calls for a word of caution. Shoghi Effendi, in a letter written on his behalf, has stated that "Bahá'u'lláh has made it clear enough that only those things that have been revealed in the form of Tablets have a binding power over the friends. Hearsays may be matters of interest but can in no way claim authority. . . . This being a basic principle of the Faith we should not confuse Tablets that were actually revealed and mere talks attributed to the Founders of the Cause. The first have absolute binding authority while the latter can in no way claim our obedience. The highest thing this can achieve is to influence the activities of one who has heard the saying in person."

Thus the nature of our response to the varied sources is clear. For the binding words of 'Abdu'l-Bahá and Shoghi Effendi one should go to the authorized, published texts. The hearsays or remembrances of 'Abdu'l-Bahá, filtered through the experiences and interpretations of the early Bahá'ís who met Him, one should place in a distinctly separate, nonbinding category. Yet such memoirs—including such works as Howard Colby Ives's *Portals to Freedom*, May Maxwell's *An Early Pilgrimage*, Helen Goodall's and Ella Cooper's *Daily Lessons Received at 'Akká*, and Julia Grundy's *Ten Days in the Light of 'Akká*—all give one a sense of the vibrancy, of the love and patience, of the foresight and wisdom of 'Abdu'l-Bahá. Such accounts are not binding, to be sure; but they are treasures of the early days of the Bahá'í Faith, priceless accounts of how 'Abdu'l-Bahá's words influenced the lives of the authors. With Ramona Brown sometimes it was not even 'Abdu'l-Bahá's words that drew her to Him: "As He looked into my eyes, His gentle smiling eyes touched my soul; they seemed to tell me that He knew what was in my heart and everything about me. I felt as though I were in another world. At that moment I silently gave my heart and dedicated my life to Him." *Memories of 'Abdu'l-Bahá* is an account of the dedication of Ramona Brown and of that intrepid band of Bahá'ís she encountered in California, the lives of whom stand as testaments to the lasting and far-reaching effects of 'Abdu'l-Bahá's words and Tablets and to their devotion to the Cause of Bahá'u'lláh.

Preface

In February 1969 the Hand of the Cause of God William Sears asked me to "write everything you can remember" about being with 'Abdu'l-Bahá when He visited California in 1912 and about the early history of the Bahá'í Faith in the Oakland area. Mr. Sears later reminded me that this material would be "very important and valuable because people are starving for stories about 'Abdu'l-Bahá and the early days."

This book is not intended to be a complete record of the early days of the Bahá'í Faith in California. Rather, it is a personal account of some of the most important and inspiring events, written by one who participated in those history-making decades when the Faith was being established in the West and when 'Abdu'l-Bahá visited here. I have included additional material as background and for the enjoyment of the reader. It is my wish to record these recollections before they are lost to future generations, so that others may share in the knowledge and beauty of those glorious times.

I would like to pay tribute to the truly steadfast and dedicated Bahá'ís who introduced and taught the Faith in those early days in the Bay Area. In his powerful book *The World Order of Bahá'u'lláh* Shoghi Effendi said of some of the early American friends: "I can never pay sufficient tribute to that spirit of unyielding determination which the impact of a magnetic personality ['Abdu'l-Bahá] and the spell of a mighty utterance kindled in the entire company of these returning pilgrims, these consecrated heralds of the Covenant of God. . . ."[1] 'Abdu'l-Bahá gave special titles to some of them. He called Helen Goodall the "Spiritual Mother of the Oakland Community"; Lua Getsinger, "Mother Teacher of the West"; and Phoebe Hearst, "Mother of the Faithful."[2] Other teachers were Ella Goodall Cooper, Kathryn Frankland, Ella Bailey, Frances Allen, Hyde Dunn, Isabella Brittingham, Emogene Hoagg, Mary H. Ford, Thornton Chase, Willard Hatch, Agnes Alexander, Martha Root, Mírzá Abu'l-Faḍl, and Ali-Kuli Khan.

Mírzá Abu'l-Faḍl was sent by 'Abdu'l-Bahá to teach in America. The Master wrote of him to an American believer: "Verily, his visit is a prize unto thee . . . a consolation unto thy heart and a joy unto thy soul and thou wilt gain from him wisdom and explanation in conformity with evident facts and ocular demonstration."[3] Abu'l-Faḍl departed from this world January 22, 1914, in Cairo, Egypt.[4]

Ali-Kuli Khan was the great Persian scholar and translator who served as amanuensis to 'Abdu'l-Bahá in 'Akká. Later, with his family, he lived and taught in Washington, D.C., and in many cities in America. He was one of the most learned teachers of the Faith.

I am especially grateful to Bijou Straun, who took notes at numerous meetings and gave me copies of many of the Master's talks. Bijou was a small, slight young woman who walked very fast and was always in a hurry. She usually had several books and papers under her arm. A pleasant person with an easy laugh, Bijou was very quick in her speech, alert in her thinking, extremely energetic, and efficient in recording 'Abdu'l-Bahá's many lectures and talks in California. Although she was employed, she always managed willingly and eagerly to serve Him and the Faith.

One of the early believers said: "In 'Abdu'l-Bahá's presence one gains an insight of the great wisdom Bahá'u'lláh had to establish the Kingdom of God in this day. Hearts must be turned to God, and this is their desire and choice. Constant training and studying are necessary to keep the souls in the straight path, so naturally His chosen instruments for that purpose must be perfect in qualities, wisdom, and judgment." One reason the early believers who established the Faith in California were so happy was due to their strict obedience to the Teachings of 'Abdu'l-Bahá and their determination and effort never to compromise the Faith.

Acknowledgment

I wish to acknowledge with deep and loving gratitude the devoted assistance of Kay Patton in the preparation of this manuscript. Without her cheerful encouragement and great, loving effort these recollections might never have been written.

Part 1

*Early Believers
in California*

Early Believers in California

Verily, I saw your photographs, whose beauty proved the turning of your hearts unto the Center of Guidance and the dilation of your breasts by the appearance of the Kingdom of God. The light of God is verily shining in the face of the man who is of the Kingdom, spiritual, heavenly, divine and Bahai. . . .

Thank God for that He enlightened your faces by the light of guidance, deposited in your hearts the sign of faith, and made you of the chosen ones in this new century.

'Abdu'l-Bahá[1]

"Marhabá! Marhabá!" ("Welcome! Welcome!"), then "Are you happy? Are you happy?"—these were the cheery words of greeting we heard in 'Abdu'l-Bahá's ringing voice as He entered the hall of the home He had rented in San Francisco, where a group of us had been awaiting His return from a walk in the morning sunshine. I shall always remember that startling moment, the excitement I felt on hearing His happy voice, and the pleasure of being in the presence of the Master. It is one of my most cherished recollections.

Many memories of 'Abdu'l-Bahá's visit to California in 1912 crowd my mind. I vividly recall the many precious and wonderful moments, the blessed and happy occasions when I was with Him. I am mindful, too, of the truly steadfast and dedicated Bahá'ís who established the Faith of Bahá'u'lláh in Oakland in 1898 and later in San

Francisco and other cities of the Bay Area. We owe deep gratitude to those friends who spent their lives in the service of the Faith, for without them we in California might not have known much about the Revelation of Bahá'u'lláh at that time or in this day.

It was Helen Goodall who opened her beautiful home in the early days of the Faith in Oakland so that the friends could meet to investigate the Teachings. Many meetings and Feasts took place there over the years. Helen was a lady of great sweetness and dignity, with a soft, pleasing voice and a modest and gracious manner. One felt her deep humility when she spoke of Bahá'u'lláh and 'Abdu'l-Bahá. She was a slender person with snow-white hair. Her serene smile revealed her tranquil heart. Quiet inner strength enabled her to carry on her many activities. Helen exemplified the truly charming and genteel qualities of a lady of that time. In her association with the many people who attended the meetings in her home, she had the unique gift of making everyone feel welcome, comfortable, and happy.

Ella Goodall Cooper was Helen's daughter. Ella was one of the self-sacrificing souls who gave freely of themselves to establish the Faith in Oakland and the San Francisco Bay Area. She was my spiritual teacher, and it was she who inspired my love and understanding of the Faith. We were devoted friends always. Everyone felt Ella's happy exuberance when she entered a room. She had a charm and a beautiful, loving spirit which drew friends to her. Her loyalty and kindness endeared her to her many friends throughout the years.

Phoebe Hearst was a friend of Helen and Ella; it was Ann Apperson, a niece of Phoebe's, who first told Helen and Ella about the Bahá'í Faith. Shortly afterwards, in 1898, Lua, Helen, and Ella were so interested in this new Faith that they went to New York to study further with the Bahá'í teacher Anṭún Ḥaddád.[2]

In 1904 my family lived on Ashby Avenue in Berkeley, where my brother, Warren, and I were raised. In that year my mother, Frances Orr Allen, and I were invited by a friend, Mrs. Anna Monroe, to meet Helen Goodall and her daughter, Ella. That was the most important day of my life. I was fifteen years of age.

Mrs. Goodall had a large, elegant home in Oakland at 1537 Jackson Street. The day we went to her home for tea the imposing door was opened by a Japanese servant with a brilliant smile. He was Yamamoto. About a year later Helen and Ella gave a beautiful wedding for him and his bride when she arrived from Japan; I still have the little gold wedding ring which my mother found in her piece of wedding cake. Kanichi Yamamoto became the first Japanese Bahá'í in the world [in 1902], and some of his children are Bahá'ís. Of Yamamoto, who heard of the Faith in Honolulu, 'Abdu'l-Bahá said, "thou . . . art the single one of Japan and the unique one of the extreme Orient."[3] Yamamoto remained a staunch and ardent Bahá'í, continuing in Helen's service for many years.

That memorable afternoon Yamamoto led us into the spacious reception hall of the Goodall home. Helen and Ella came forward and greeted us with the most radiant smiles I had ever seen. We were strangers; yet they met us with a warm welcome full of love. We were seated in the lovely dining room, and tea was served. Then they began telling us about 'Abdu'l-Bahá. It was the first time we had heard the word *Bahá'í*. They spoke of the Master's many years with His Father in prison, and of His exile and the cruel treatment of Bahá'u'lláh and His Family because of the opposition of the Persian and Turkish governments. They told us of 'Abdu'l-Bahá's daily life, of His deeds, of His deprivations of all worldly comforts, and of His kindness to all, rich and poor. They told us how the Master daily visited the sick and gave gifts to the poor, and also how some of those poor people would cover their palms with their cloaks to avoid contact with Him when receiving His gifts and after receiving them would spit at Him. Helen and Ella described 'Abdu'l-Bahá's happiness and light spirit showering His love over all, friends and ill-wishers alike, despite His imprisonment and the difficult conditions under which He and His Family lived.

Their story fascinated me, for I had a great longing to learn about God and to find answers concerning how God could reach and teach His people. My parents understood this longing for spiritual knowledge, and they allowed me to attend various Sunday schools in my search. At last, at one of the Sunday schools, I found a warm-hearted, loving teacher, Mrs. Anderson, who understood my search. She told me that at different times in history God sent a special Teacher to the people of the world to guide them. She told me about Jesus and said that He was one of God's special Messengers. She described His way of life, gave His Teachings of brotherly love, and then explained the great sacrifice He made to awaken the people to turn to God, to love Him, and obey His commands. I was very happy because I had found the answer to my questions, and I knew then that God had a plan and would always provide a spiritual Teacher to guide the people.

I sat spellbound, listening to those friends speaking about this wonderful Person, 'Abdu'l-Bahá, so much like Jesus, both of Them sacrificing Themselves and calling all mankind to love and peace. I had finally found that for which I had been searching. I turned to my mother and said, "I believe this!", for I had instantly accepted Bahá'u'lláh and His Teachings and knew that 'Abdu'l-Bahá was the spiritual Teacher for this day Whom I had been longing to find all of my life. At last, I had attained my heart's desire, and throughout my life I have never had any doubts. From that day on I have shared this wonderful Message with my friends and with people I have met wherever I have been.

No printed Bahá'í books were available in the early days. When we attended a Feast and were seated at a table, at each place was a slip of paper on which a different verse from *The Hidden Words of Bahá'u'lláh* had been typewritten. These we read in turn. Several years later we received a very few published copies of *The Hidden Words*. Many of the Teachings were sent as Tablets and prayers from 'Abdu'l-Bahá to Mrs. Goodall, who had them copied for the early believers. It took many weeks for Messages from 'Abdu'l-Bahá to come from Haifa by boat. One of those rare Tablets follows:

> To the maidservant of God, Helen S. Goodall
> Upon her be Bahá'u'lláh!
> He is God!
> O thou who art attracted by the Fragrances of God! Verily I read thy recent letter, dated October 30, 1902, and noted its contents which indicated the sincerity of thy heart, thy exceeding joy, thy great longing for the Kingdom of God, and thy endeavor in the diffusion of the Fragrances of God.
>
> Blessed art thou for guiding certain souls unto the Kingdom of God and giving them to drink of the wine of the Love of God from the Chalice of His Guidance.
>
> As to thy question concerning the "Minor Resurrection" and the first creation: this is the appearance of the Báb, the Great, His Holiness the Supreme. But the Major Resurrection signifies the Manifestation of the Preexistent Beauty (Bahá'u'lláh), the Greatest Name (May my spirit be a sacrifice for His beloved!).
>
> By the Majesty of My Lord, verily, your gathering in the meeting of Oneness, your commemoration of God with a pure heart, and your association with a spirit, rejoicing by the Spirit of God in this Great Day, profiteth you more than all favors, and this Bounty surpasseth all wishes.
>
> O maidservant of God! Neglect not even for a moment to commemorate God. Assemble the maidservants of the Merciful, with all spirituality and fragrance, love and attraction, and raise your voice in praise and glory to your Majestic Lord for His abundant Mercy and great favor of Guidance. . . .
> Upon thee be greeting and praise
> (signed) 'Abdu'l-Bahá 'Abbás[4]

The early followers had only a few prayers and teachings, but the unity and harmony among them flourished because of the power of the Holy Spirit and their love for Bahá'u'lláh and the Master. The friends were drawn together by the spiritual message and the true expressions of love and fellowship among the believers gathered at the meetings. The examples of true Bahá'í living and deeds set before us by Helen and Ella were our guide. Fortunate indeed were the friends who lived through those pioneer days of the Faith under their guidance. 'Abdu'l-Bahá Himself addressed Helen Goodall as the "Spiritual Mother of This Confirmed Community."

Ella Goodall was one of the earliest Westerners to visit the Master when she went on pilgrimage to 'Akká with Phoebe Hearst in 1898.[5] It was during that visit that 'Abdu'l-Bahá revealed the first of numerous Tablets which He sent to her over the succeeding years:

> He is Al-Abhá!
> O my God! Thou seest Thy servant who is believing in Thee, and supplicating through the door of Thy Oneness. Render her all good through Thy Bounty and Generosity. Thou art the Bestower, the Giver.[6]

Ella gave me a copy of the following Tablet which she received December 30, 1905, from the Master: "O maidservant of God! Hasten and sow the seed as best you can, for time passes away, and through it shall the blessing of the Kingdom appear."[7]

'Abdu'l-Bahá sent another Tablet to a friend of Ella's in which He mentioned both Helen and Ella:

> Thou hadst written concerning the services of Mrs. Goodall and Mrs. Cooper. These two dear maidservants of God are truly two shining candles and in character are unique and matchless. They sacrifice their lives in the pathway of God under all conditions of hardships and are filled with spirituality and good cheer. It is certain that the divine confirmations will attend them.

When Ella married Dr. Charles Minor Cooper in 1904,

HELEN GOODALL
called by 'Abdu'l-Bahá the "Spiritual Mother of the [Oakland] Confirmed Community," standing in the garden of the Master's home in Haifa in 1920.

Home of Helen Goodall at 1537 Jackson Street, Oakland, California, where Bahá'í meetings were held around 1900.

ELLA GOODALL COOPER
addressed by 'Abdu'l-Bahá as "Jewel of the Spirit"
and termed by Shoghi Effendi a herald of the Covenant and
a "dearly loved handmaid" of 'Abdu'l-Bahá.

at whose home were held the first Bahá'í meetings in Berkeley, California.

FRANCES ORR ALLEN
DR. WOODSON ALLEN

LUA GETSINGER
named by 'Abdu'l-Bahá a "Herald of the Covenant" and
by Shoghi Effendi the "Mother Teacher of the West."

PHOEBE APPERSON HEARST
called by 'Abdu'l-Bahá the "Mother of the Faithful."

AGNES ALEXANDER and MAY BOLLES (MAXWELL) shown together in Portland, Oregon, in 1924.

they moved from Oakland to San Francisco. After the great earthquake and fire of 1906 Ella and her husband returned to live with Helen and her son, Arthur, in Oakland. Meetings continued to be held in the Goodall home even after the earthquake, and as the interest grew among their group of friends, others held meetings in their homes in Berkeley, Fruitvale, and Hayward. By 1906 there were Bahá'í groups in Oakland, Berkeley, San Francisco, and nearby cities. Automobiles were coming into existence, so that it was easier for the friends to attend meetings.

My parents, Dr. Woodson and Frances Allen, were deeply interested in the Faith and received Tablets from 'Abdu'l-Bahá. One of the many Tablets written to my mother was this one:

He is God!

O! Thou dear maidservant of God! Your letter was received and its contents became known. Have no care because of the blame of enemies and the remonstrance of relatives. For this is in the path of God, and this will bring you honor in both worlds. During all the former cycles—the cycle of Abraham, the cycle of Moses, the cycle of Christ—men and women believers have always been objects of blame on the part of the heedless ones, but before long the situation was reversed. Blame was changed into praise, and remonstrance was changed into glorification, and they received great commendation and exaltation. Those who were the relatives and had persecuted them began to honor them, praising God that they were related to such believers and were the kin of those who had been guided by the light of Guidance.

Accordingly you too be assured that before long all blame shall cease and all reproach shall pass away and all will praise and glorify you.

. . . .

You had written concerning the meetings held at Mrs. Goodall's home. These will undoubtedly produce great results and manifest important effects, and these will promote love and unity amongst men and will bring about the oneness of mankind.

As to Mrs. Bailey, if she was relieved from life in this mortal world, she attained immortal life. If she was departed from this earthly plane, she hastened to the world of the Kingdom. Be thou assured, and rejoice that she is submerged in the sea of forgiveness and received immortal life in the Kingdom of God.

O maidservant of God! I hope through the Grace and Bounty of the Creator that the lights of guidance may shine upon the members of that household (family) and that they may receive a portion from the bounty of the Kingdom.

Upon thee be BAHÁ-Al-Abhá!
(signed by 'Abdu'l-Bahá)[8]

To the home of my parents came many of the early teachers of the Faith: Lua Getsinger, Mary Hanford Ford, Willard Hatch, Thornton Chase, Isabella Brittingham, Helen Goodall, Ella Cooper, Ali-Kuli Khan, Martha Root, Hyde Dunn, and his wife, Clara. Some of them spent weekends in our home. The first Bahá'í meetings were held there, and that was where my mother invited her friends to hear Lua Getsinger speak about the Faith.

Lua Getsinger contributed much to my love for 'Abdu'l-Bahá and the Bahá'í Faith. Lua was born November 1, 1871, on a farm in upstate New York.[9] At an early age she began studying music and drama, expecting to have a career in these fields. Yet soon after she heard about the Bahá'í Faith, in 1893 at the World Congress in Chicago, she gave up all thoughts of a career and devoted the rest of her life to teaching the Cause.[10]

Before the arrival of 'Abdu'l-Bahá in California, Lua often spent weekends in our home at 2718 Webster Street in Berkeley, where my mother arranged meetings so that her friends could meet Lua and hear her speak. Lua had been especially instructed by the Master to give His explanations of many subjects and clarify numerous points; we were deeply grateful for this bounty since in those days we had no Bahá'í books from which to study.

Lua enjoyed being in our home with "her family" as she called us. I remember that she liked to sit in the corner of a room so that she could look into the face of each person while she spoke. Lua was a lovely portrait in her blue costume. She had pretty brown hair, ivory skin, naturally red lips, and blue eyes which were accentuated by a soft blue scarf falling from her hat across her shoulders. A celestial radiance seemed to surround her as she spoke with a simplicity and charm that attracted many people to the Faith.

Lua had at one time enjoyed wearing beautiful, fashionable clothes. She told me that one day when she was in 'Akká, 'Abdu'l-Bahá sent for her and showed her a sketch He had drawn of simple wearing apparel. He instructed her to have garments made like those in the sketch and from that time on to wear them. One of Lua's outstanding virtues was her strict obedience to 'Abdu'l-Bahá's slightest wish; so she had the garments made. The dress was a lovely shade of dark royal blue—with a matching wrap, like an 'abá, for summer, and for winter a long coat of the same color, trimmed with velvet collar and cuffs. From the sides and back of a small, round hat, of a matching blue, silky material, a full scarf fell to her waist. Later on she told me that the unusual blue costume had proved to be a safeguard to her during hazardous experiences in many countries as she traveled in service to the Faith.

Lua was the guest of the Master in 'Akká several times. She told me that once she was terribly ill there and that 'Abdu'l-Bahá sent her an apple, instructing her to eat it. Despite the opinion that no one with her illness should eat apples, she obeyed; and by the next day she had completely recovered.[11]

While Lua and Dr. Getsinger were in 'Akká with the [first] party of [Western] pilgrims, the Master put something into her mouth, saying: "'I have given you the power to speak and loosened your tongue. "Lua" in Persian means "Flag" and you must be my flag and wave it in the East and the West.'" Dr. Getsinger recalled that

'Abdu'l-Bahá then gave an exhortation "into which he put such spiritual force and emphasis that it seemed as though the very walls trembled and we were hardly able to stand on our feet. Abdul-Baha was declaring that the millennium had come and the Kingdom of God was to be established on earth. He wanted Lua thus to proclaim it everywhere in a loud voice."[12]

'Abdu'l-Bahá said to the early Bahá'ís: "Assuredly ye will achieve a Conquest in California."[13] In 1911 'Abdu'l-Bahá sent Lua and one of His secretaries to California, to San Diego, La Jolla, and Point Loma, and to Tijuana, Mexico, to spread the Bahá'í Teachings. The United States [naval] fleet was stationed in San Diego harbor, and on the battleship *California*, the flagship [of the fleet], a large meeting was held for the crew. Mr. Mack, who received the message at that time, then held meetings in his cabin. Some of his friends who attended were later transferred to other ships where they spread news of the Revelation of Bahá'u'lláh. Lua spoke at the Women's City Club in San Diego, and meetings were held in two men's clubs, in halls, and in private homes. Some of the citizens, a few of them prominent, became interested; and Bahá'í groups were formed.

From San Diego [and La Jolla] believers went to small outlying cities and towns. Through the perseverence of those devoted and dedicated souls large communities thrive today in San Diego and surrounding cities, where Local Spiritual Assemblies have been formed. There are now also many believers in Tijuana and a Spiritual Assembly there and in several other Mexican cities along the border. One of the first Bahá'ís in Tijuana, Esperanza de Herrera y Puerto, has given property for a House of Worship to be built in the future on a foothill overlooking that beautiful coastal metropolis where Lua Getsinger first brought the Teachings of Bahá'u'lláh.

On June 6, 1920, in Haifa, 'Abdu'l-Bahá revealed for the friends a special prayer for the city of San Diego:

> O Thou the Lord of Hosts! The city of San Diego was like a lifeless body. Now a breath of the Spirit of Life has

wafted over those regions. Some souls have arisen from the graves of the world of nature which is the eternal death; they have been revived by the Holy Ghost, and they have started in servitude to Thy threshold.

O Thou affectionate Lord! Bestow upon these featherless and wingless birds two heavenly wings and give unto them spiritual strength, so that they may soar in the limitless space and attain to the apex of the Kingdom of Abha!

O Lord! Strengthen these feeble seedlings so that each one may develop into a fruitful tree, exhibiting the utmost freshness and liveliness. Assist them and make them victorious, so that they may rout and vanquish the army of ignorance and misapprehension; lift up the banner of love and guidance among the people; bestow like unto the spring breeze freshness and life unto the tree of humanity; give greenness and liveliness like unto the spring shower to the meadows of that continent! Verily, Thou art the Able and the Powerful, the Bestower and the Affectionate![14]

Lua and I became very good friends, and she called me her "little Persian sister." I often visited her in her hotel in San Francisco. Many times when we were together, teaching problems would arise, and decisions would have to be made. I remember once when Lua was asked to speak in a city south of San Francisco, and the question arose as to whether to spend the money for the trip or buy a pair of shoes for a very needy Bahá'í. We considered the question and prayed sincerely while holding a volume of my book *Tablets of Abdul-Baha*, which I then opened for guidance. The decision was reached that the shoes were to be bought. Another time Lua did not know whether to stay in town (San Francisco) or go to Palo Alto to teach. We prayed, and I opened my book and read, "The path has been cleared, the way opened for her." Lua went to Palo Alto to teach.

One morning, when some of us were in 'Abdu'l-Bahá's residence in San Francisco, Lua told me that she and I were to have an interview with the Master. As Lua spoke Persian very well, we did not need an interpreter. She told 'Abdu'l-Bahá about our friendship, which seemed to please Him. Then she showed Him my book and explained that, when we had a problem, we would use it, after meditation and prayer, as a means of guidance. 'Abdu'l-Bahá was very interested and attentive. He smiled at me and said: "You have intuition. You must follow it always, because when you follow it, it increases and becomes more clear. Only a few have this gift. It is like the tinkling of bells, a sixth sense, like the voice of God speaking. The more one follows intuition, the more it increases."

Lua asked the Master if I might use the book for guidance in the future. Smiling at me, He said, "Yes." Then He took my book, opened it, and, resting it on the palm of His left hand, wrote His name in it. Afterwards He gave me a beautiful, fragrant red rose. Some of the petals still cling to the book above His signature.

Our visit with 'Abdu'l-Bahá being over, Lua left the room. As I started to leave, I turned for one last look at His beautiful face, for I wanted to remember that moment always. Suddenly He walked to a door, opened it, and from a shelf took a little bag out of which He gave me two lovely Bahá'í ringstones, one for my father and one for my friend Joseph Bray. About two years later 'Abdu'l-Bahá sent me a wonderful gift from the Holy Land: a light carnelian Bahá'í ringstone and pink prayer beads.

One afternoon, shortly before Lua left San Francisco in 1912, we were having an especially happy time recalling the wonderful hours we had spent together. Suddenly a strange feeling came over me as though I were about to witness a crisis. Lua walked to her bureau, opened a drawer, and took out a box. Lovingly she smiled at me and put it in my hand, saying, "This is for you, Mona dear." Happily I received her gift and opened the box. There, carefully wrapped, lay a beautiful pair of long white kid gloves. Instinctively I knew this gift was the last remnant of her lovely clothes, which she had always enjoyed, and the symbol of her complete detachment from worldly things. I was deeply touched.

When the Master went to New York, Lua traveled with the group. She told me that it was in New York City that 'Abdu'l-Bahá first taught the American Bahá'ís about the protecting power of obedience to the Covenant of Bahá'u'lláh. There, on June 19, 1912, when the friends were gathered in the basement of His house, the translation of the "Tablet of the Branch" was read for the first time in this country. It is for this reason that New York is called the "City of the Covenant."[15]

On that day 'Abdu'l-Bahá was upstairs sitting while Juliet Thompson painted His portrait. Lua was seated nearby, and Juliet said to her: "I think the Master is asleep! Perhaps we should let Him sleep." With those words 'Abdu'l-Bahá opened His eyes and in a powerful voice said to Lua "I appoint you the Herald of the Covenant. Go down and tell the people I am the Center of the Covenant!" The whole world must have shaken at those electrifying words. Lua hesitated and with tears streaming down her face said, "O Lord, not I! O my Lord, recreate me!" He repeated His command to her, and she went down to proclaim to the friends the station of 'Abdu'l-Bahá.[16]

The believers were so filled with love for the Master that they wanted very much to celebrate His birthday and asked His permission to do this. He replied that, as His birthday falls on the same day as the Declaration of the Báb (May 23), and He did not want to detract from the glory of that day, He would like the friends instead to celebrate November 26 as the Day of the Covenant. Ever since then this day has been celebrated as one of the Bahá'í holy days.

Lua was sent on many important missions by the Master. One time she went to see the Sháh of Persia with a petition requesting the Sháh to put an end to the martyrdoms of Bahá'ís in his country. The Sháh's son was desperately ill, and his minister made an agreement with Lua that if the boy was healed he would stop the martyrdoms. Lua called on Bahá'í friends to join her in healing prayers, which they said all night. In the morning Lua returned to the Sháh's palace and found that his son was getting well. The Sháh kept the promise, and the cruelties eased for awhile.[17]

It was said of Lua that she was a comfort to the poor and an example to the rich. She traveled extensively, often with Mírzá Abu'l-Faḍl, teaching the Faith in many parts of the world. Even ill health did not deter her. Dr. Getsinger tells us that 'Abdu'l-Bahá said after one of her illnesses, "I told the angel of death to 'stay away.'"[18]

In a letter from 'Abdu'l-Bahá written August 19, 1913, in Ramlih, Egypt, Lua received the following instructions:

> Thou must be firm and unshakable in thy purpose, and never, never let any outward circumstances worry thee. I am sending thee to India to accomplish certain definite results. Thou must enter that country with a never-failing spirituality, a radiant faith, an eternal enthusiasm, an inextinguishable fire, a solid conviction, in order that thou mayest achieve those services for which I am sending thee. Let not thy heart be troubled. If thou goest away with this unchanging condition of invariability of inner state, thou shalt see the doors of confirmation open before thy face, thy life will be a crown of heavenly roses, and thou shalt find thyself in the highest station of triumph.
>
> . . . Thou dost not know a thousandth part of the difficulties and seemingly unsurmountable passes that rise daily before my eyes. I do not heed them; I am walking in my chosen highway; I know the destination.[19]

Just before Lua left San Francisco she gave me a little silver teapot from which she had often served me tea. When I use it, I recall Lua and the many happy hours we spent together.

In 1913 I received a letter from her in which she enclosed the following Tablet and note:

He is God!
To the presence of the Hon. Lua M. Getsinger
(46th from the year of Dawning)

> O thou shining and spiritual Gem!
> Glad tidings to thee from the Generosity of Thy Lord.
> Be happy on account of the Gifts of thy God which shall soon surround thee; and Thou art confirmed in the Covenant!
>
> Abdul Baha Abbas

Revealed in 'Akká in 1898 and sent to Haifa where I was staying after my first meeting with the Beloved. It was my *first* Tablet!   Lua

Lua passed away May 1, 1916, in Cairo, Egypt, and is buried in the Bahá'í cemetery close to the tomb of Mírzá Abu'l-Faḍl. When 'Abdu'l-Bahá was informed of Lua's death, He said sadly: "What a loss! What a loss!"

One of Lua Getsinger's first students of the Bahá'í Faith was Phoebe Hearst. Phoebe was born in St. Clair, Missouri, December 3, 1844.[20] She came to California with her husband, George, in the very early days. Immediately after hearing the Message of Bahá'u'lláh [in 1898] Phoebe felt impelled to make a pilgrimage to 'Akká to meet 'Abdu'l-Bahá. In December 1898 she organized a group of fourteen friends to make a pilgrimage.[21] The group included her niece, Ann Apperson, Lua and her husband, Dr. Edward Getsinger, Ella Goodall, Nellie Hillyer, and May Bolles. Phoebe afterwards related in a letter, "those three days [in 'Akká] were the most memorable days of my life."[22]

Because of the danger to 'Abdu'l-Bahá in having visitors, especially from the West, the party separated into three groups. I recall Ella's account of her trip and of sailing on the Nile River with Nellie Hillyer while waiting for their turn to go to 'Akká.

During those days 'Abdu'l-Bahá was still a prisoner of the Turkish government because of political and religious prejudices against Bahá'u'lláh's Teachings. Great care had to be taken so that news of the growth of the Faith of Bahá'u'lláh in the Western world would not reach the Turkish government, for it would have greatly endangered the life of 'Abdu'l-Bahá. He was allowed little freedom, and He showed the strain of years of imprisonment and deprivations. This group of loving friends from America gave great happiness and comfort to the Master and the Greatest Holy Leaf. These Western pilgrims arrived [six years] after the ascension of Bahá'u'lláh at a time when severe trials and hardships were increasing for the Holy Family. The presence of these pilgrims seemed to encourage them and help them survive the ordeals which they must endure then and in the future.

May Bolles Maxwell later wrote the story of that pilgrimage and mentioned that, when the group visited the resting place of Bahá'u'lláh, 'Abdu'l-Bahá said: "'We are now going to visit the Holy Tomb. When you are praying in that divine spot remember the promise of Bahá'u'lláh, that those who attain this pilgrimage shall receive an answer to their prayers, and their wishes shall be granted.'"[23] May became a Bahá'í shortly after that pilgrimage and served the Faith for forty years.[24] Her daughter, Mary Maxwell, became Amatu'l-Bahá Rúḥíyyih Khánum, the wife of Shoghi Effendi.

In recognition of May's outstanding work in South America Shoghi Effendi named her "The Mother Teacher of the Latin People." On March 1, 1940, May gave her life while teaching in Buenos Aires, and the Guardian cabled the believers: "To sacred tie her signal services had forged, the priceless honor of a martyr's crown is now added. . . ."[25]

It was on this trip with Phoebe Hearst that Robert Turner, a servant of Phoebe's who had accompanied her, became the first Negro Bahá'í in the West.[26] On the day of the arrival of the pilgrims at the home of 'Abdu'l-Bahá in 'Akká, when dinner was to be served, 'Abdu'l-Bahá noticed that no place at the table had been set for Robert. Instead, it appeared that he would be expected to help serve. Going to find Robert, the Master brought him to the table, seated him in His place, and proceeded to serve the friends Himself.[27]

After Phoebe returned from 'Akká, she attended

Bahá'í meetings [in the Bay Area] and invited her friends to her home in Pleasanton to learn about the Faith. She also had a penthouse apartment in San Francisco. Often when Lua would visit her there, tired and hungry after a late meeting, Phoebe would send out for oyster stew. While they enjoyed the stew, Lua would deepen Phoebe in the Bahá'í Teachings. Phoebe was fascinated by Lua's vibrant spirit and her eloquence. Lua's sincere and deep desire was to herald the Kingdom of God. One of Lua's secrets of successful teaching was that she held her pupils close to her until they were firmly grounded in the Teachings.

It was my pleasure to be a guest in Phoebe's home in 1910 before 'Abdu'l-Bahá's visit there. Phoebe was the wife of Senator George F. Hearst. She was a very conservative, genteel lady. She was interested in young people and enjoyed entertaining them in her home. Once when I was visiting her at the Hacienda, as she called her home in Pleasanton, her niece, Agnes Lane, and Louise Herron were guests there also. One day the two girls went to San Francisco "on a lark." When they came in to dinner that evening, they appeared to be wearing earrings. Phoebe, who did not approve of young ladies wearing earrings, started to rebuke the girls when to our astonishment they laughingly removed the earrings and ate them. The earrings were little gumdrops. We all laughed at their trick.

Phoebe never lost her interest in the Cause or her contact with the Bahá'ís of California. 'Abdu'l-Bahá gave her the title of "Mother of the Faithful." In a letter dated November 19, 1899, to Mr. I. H. Bradford, she wrote: "I believe with all my heart that He is the Master and my greatest blessing in this world is that I have been privileged to be in His presence and look upon His sanctified face." In a letter dated December 5 of that same year Phoebe wrote to Mr. O. M. Babcock: "It seems to me a real Truthseeker would know at a glance that He is the Master! Withal, I must say He is the Most Wonderful Being I have ever met or ever expect to meet in this world."[28]

Besides educating her own son, William Randolph, Phoebe educated and helped many other young people. A cofounder of the [National Congress of] Parents and Teachers, she was very active in educational and cultural affairs. She gave to the University of California at Berkeley the magnificent Hearst [Memorial] Mining Building, Hearst Hall for girls, and the Museum of Anthropology.[29] In addition to other donations to the University of California Phoebe outfitted and maintained archeological expeditions in Egypt [and elsewhere] and gave immeasurable assistance to the Panama Pacific International Exposition. The extent of her private charities will never be known. Phoebe's interest in education and her cooperation with individuals and educational organizations will keep her memory fresh for those who knew and loved her and will greatly benefit future generations.

In July 1916, at the age of seventy-two, Phoebe walked the entire distance in the Preparedness Parade in San Francisco. On April 5, 1919, Phoebe passed away in her home, La Hacienda.[30] At the 1969 Charter Day Exhibition at the University of California at Berkeley, on the fiftieth anniversary of her death, numerous pictures and articles about Phoebe were shown, and many appeared throughout the nation in newspapers and magazines. Another outstanding tribute to her was given in April 1969 by Mr. E. H. Clark, who had attended her funeral in Grace Cathedral, San Francisco. There, on the occasion of the fiftieth anniversary of her death, Mr. Clark arranged for a special prayer to be said in her memory. On April 8, 1969, Ronald Reagan, [governor of the state of California], issued a special commendation to the memory of Phoebe Hearst and made a tape recording which paid tribute to her for her contribution to education. For over half a century the Phoebe Apperson Hearst Memorial Association has perpetuated the memory of this outstanding woman.

I am sure that Phoebe's acceptance of the Faith and her love for 'Abdu'l-Bahá, and His loving kindness to her, had an impact throughout her life. I met Phoebe in 1906, and I found her to be a loving, faithful friend and always a gracious and gallant lady. I remember Ella Cooper's telling me that near the time of Phoebe's passing she visited her at the Hacienda, and while she was holding Phoebe in her arms they repeated the Greatest Name (Yá Bahá-Al-Abhá) together; Phoebe told her that the Greatest Name had always been such a comfort to her.

After Phoebe's death the Hacienda was sold and became Castlewood Country Club. When Arthur M. Brown and I were married in 1946, we had a home in the Country Club grounds very near the Hacienda; it was a joy to me to know, as I stood on my veranda, that I was looking at the same lovely view and countryside that the Master had gazed upon and enjoyed so much when He was visiting Phoebe. Today, little remains of the Hacienda, as it was destroyed by fire on August 24, 1969; however, there still stand a small part of the exterior and a fireplace in the drawing room where 'Abdu'l-Bahá spoke with Phoebe's friends.

'Abdu'l-Bahá designated Thornton Chase, who became a Bahá'í in 1894, as " 'the first American believer.' "[31] Although he lived in Los Angeles, he was a frequent visitor in our home and often spoke at my mother's Bahá'í meetings in the early days. Thornton spread the Teachings far and wide, and his life was a worthy example to his friends and associates, to whom he spoke of the Faith with great reverence and conviction. He was a large, handsome, kindly gentleman with an engaging smile behind his long white mustache. The Master invited Thornton to make a pilgrimage to Haifa, and upon his return he wrote two books *The Bahá'í Revelation* and *In Galilee*.[32] Unfortunately, he passed away in Los Angeles on September 30, 1912, a few days before the arrival of 'Abdu'l-Bahá in California.

'Abdu'l-Bahá loved Thornton very much. On October 19 He went with a few friends from Oakland to visit Thornton's grave in Inglewood Cemetery, near Los Angeles. There He praised and extolled Thornton for his outstanding services to the Faith. The Master scattered flowers over his grave, prostrated Himself, and revealed this beautiful prayer:

> O my God! O my God! Verily, this is a servant of Thine, who did believe on Thee and in Thy signs; verily he hearkened to Thy summons, turned to Thy Kingdom, humbled himself at Thy holy threshold, was possessed of a contrite heart, arose to serve Thy cause, to spread Thy fragrances, to promote Thy word, and to expound Thy wisdom.
> Verily he guided the people to Thine ancient pathway, and led them to Thy way of rectitude. Verily he held the chalice of guidance in his right hand and gave unto those athirst to drink of the cup of favor. He presented himself at Thy lofty threshold, where he laid his brow on the fragrant soil of Thy garden and circumambulated Thy all-glorious and sublime abode, the traces of which are wide-spread and the fragrances of whose loyalty are sensed everywhere. Later he returned to these vast and extensive countries and proclaimed Thy Name amongst the people, until his respiration ceased and his outward sensation was suspended, returning to Thee with a heart throbbing with Thy love and with an eye opened to Thy direction.
> O Lord! O Lord! Submerge him in the ocean of Thy glory. O Lord! O Lord! Usher him into Thy delectable garden. O Lord! O Lord! Usher him into Thy lofty paradise and cause him to be present in Thy meeting of transfiguration. O Lord! Submerge him in the ocean of Thy lights.
> Verily, Thou art the Clement! Verily, Thou art the Merciful, the Precious, the Omnipotent![33]

Then after the prayer 'Abdu'l-Bahá spoke as follows:

> Mr. Chase was of the blessed souls. The best time of his life was spent in the path of God. He had no other aim except the good pleasure of the Lord and no other desire except the attainment to the Kingdom of God. During his lifetime he bore many trials and vicissitudes,

but he was very patient and long-suffering. He had a heart most illuminated, a spirit most rejoiced; his hope was to serve the world of humanity; during the days of his life he strove as much as he could—he never failed—until he witnessed the lights of the Kingdom of ABHA, and he was guided by the lights of Guidance. He summoned the people to the religion of God; he suffered them to enter into the Kingdom of God; he wrote books and epistles regarding the proofs and evidences of the Manifestations of BAHA'O'LLAH. In reality he has left behind him certain signs which will never be forgotten throughout ages and cycles. In reality this personage was worthy of respect. This personage is worthy of having the friends visit his grave. The traces of this personage will ever shine. This is a personage who will not be forgotten. For the present his worth is not known but in the future it will be inestimably dear. His sun will ever be shining, his stars will ever bestow the light. The people will honor this grave. Therefore, the friends of God must visit this grave and on my behalf bring flowers and seek the sublimity of the spiritual station for him and have the utmost consideration for the members of his family. This personage will not be forgotten.[34]

The Master requested that the Bahá'ís visit Thornton's grave each year; and since that time annual observances have been held, each more beautiful than the last.

Another of the early believers in California, a friend of Phoebe Hearst's, was Emogene Hoagg. Emogene was born in 1869. In 1898 she was a guest of Phoebe's at the Hacienda at Pleasanton when Lua Getsinger was invited to come and tell Phoebe and Emogene about the Faith. Emogene accepted the Teachings immediately and made her first pilgrimage to 'Akká in 1900.[35] While Helen Goodall and Ella Cooper were on a pilgrimage in 1908, Emogene conducted their Bahá'í classes in Oakland; and she also held meetings in her own home in San Francisco. Over the years Emogene traveled to many countries on teaching trips, often with Mírzá Abu'l-Faḍl.

Emogene was an accomplished pianist and also a writer, devoting much effort to a compilation which she called "The Three Conditions of Existence: Servitude, Prophethood and Deity." In 1931 Shoghi Effendi sent for Emogene to come to Haifa to type *The Dawn-Breakers*, which he was translating into English at that time.³⁶

Emogene dedicated almost every moment of her life to teaching the Faith. Her life was a shining example of the Faith she taught. After *Gleanings from the Writings of Bahá'u'lláh* was published, she would often mention at Bahá'í State Conventions and study classes the quotation from it: "let him, before all else, teach his own self, that his speech may attract the hearts of them that hear him."³⁷ Emogene was not a robust person, but she continued traveling and teaching, at last going to Charleston, South Carolina, where she was cared for by her friend, Miss Josephine Pinson. Emogene passed away there on December 15, 1945, at the age of seventy-six. She was buried in the Magnolia Cemetery in Charleston. Emogene told me that she always kept in mind the thought, " ' "It behooveth me to eliminate self . . . so that I will not desire anything but the Will of God." ' "³⁸

Georgia Grayson Ralston was a girlhood friend of Ella Goodall's. Her family had a large estate near Oakland where, as a girl, she enjoyed every luxury. She learned of the Faith from Helen and Ella Goodall [about 1910] and soon accepted the Teachings. I met Georgie while she and her husband, William Ralston (who once [in 1916] ran for governor of California), lived in the Bellevue Hotel in San Francisco. Lua also stayed there when she was in the city, and we had many wonderful and enlightening hours together as Lua expounded the Bahá'í principles.

Georgie was happy when she spoke of her efforts to advance spiritually, to acquire love for each human being, and to see God reflected in each soul. She surely reached success in her desires, for she was a sweet and loving lady of a most gentle nature.

Georgie went with Helen and Ella to New York to see 'Abdu'l-Bahá. As Georgie entered the room in the house where she was to meet Him, He stepped forward and

THORNTON CHASE
designated by 'Abdu'l-Bahá as the first American Bahá'í.

THE HACIENDA
a photograph of Phoebe Hearst's Hacienda at Pleasanton, California, taken about the time 'Abdu'l-Bahá visited there in 1912.

Views of the entrance of the Hacienda, home of Phoebe Hearst at Pleasanton, California, showing the station of the gatekeeper at the right and the entrance through which 'Abdu'l-Bahá walked during His visit of October 13–16, 1912.

photographs courtesy Ramona Brown

LUA GETSINGER and GEORGIA RALSTON

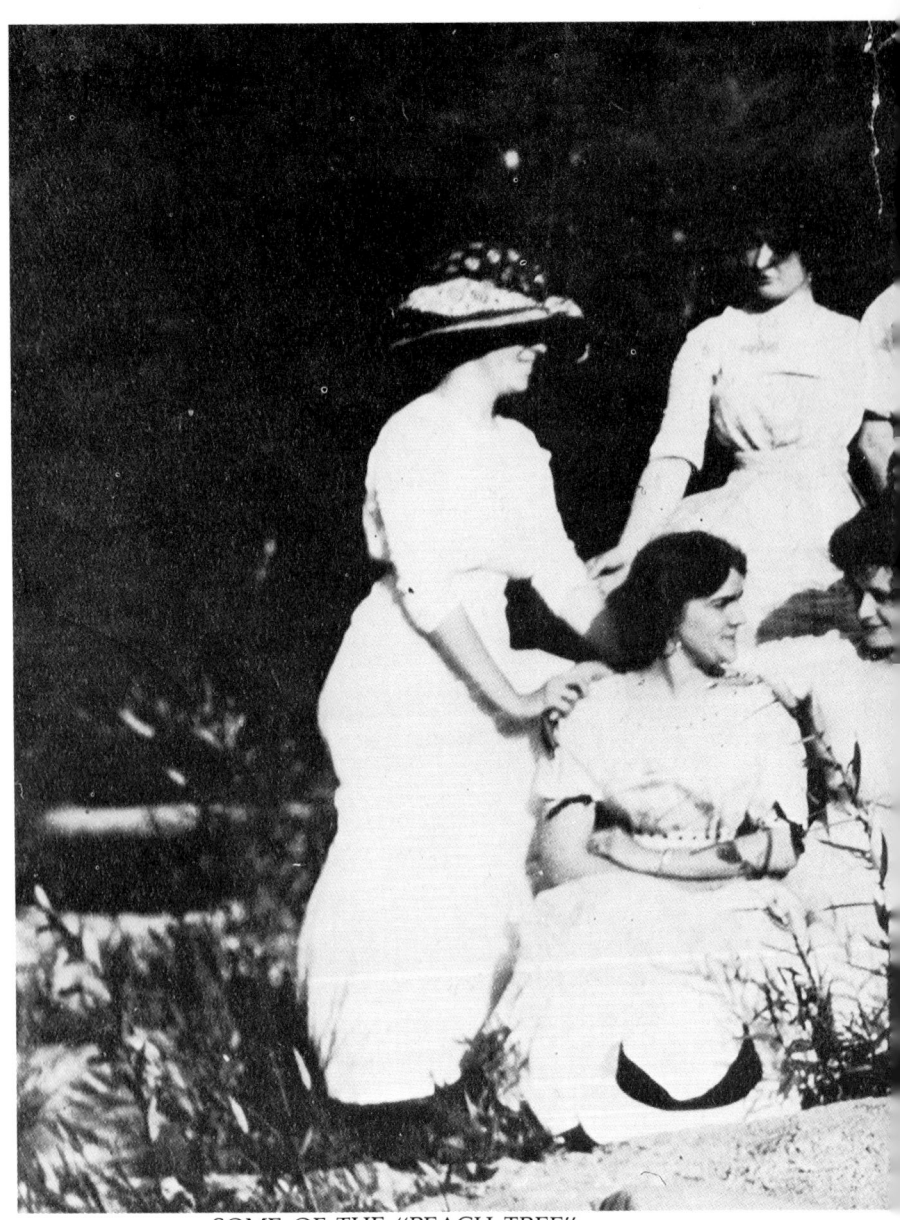
SOME OF THE "PEACH TREE"

SOME OF THE "PEACH TREE"
Front row, left to right: Ramona Allen (Bray Brown), Marie Barr (Bray), Betty Vent (Smith), and Ethel Sternberg.
Back row, left to right: Edith Woodward (Loomis), Eva Benjamin (?), Cicely Alderman (Potter), and Helen Barr (Tice).

ELLA BAILEY (right) shown (right to left) with ROBERT GULICK, MADAM FARAJU'LLAH (mother of Bahia Gulick), and RAMONA BROWN in Berkeley, California, May 7, 1950.

presented her with a large bouquet of white roses and said: "You are my daughter."[39] She told me that she was so happy and overwhelmed when He called her His daughter that she wept and wept. She said that from that moment her life was completely dedicated to Him and to the Faith. Georgie was a beautiful example of a trusting and obedient daughter throughout years of heartbreak and disappointment. She told me shortly before she died in San Francisco that her life was crowned by happiness when she made her pilgrimage in 1920 to be again in the presence of the beloved Master.

In San Francisco 'Abdu'l-Bahá liked very much to have Georgie drive Him through Golden Gate Park in her tiny electric car. It was a joy to Him to see the magnificent trees, the beautiful flowers, and the lakes in the park. Often in the early evening Georgie would drive Him up and down Market Street to see the lights, which delighted Him—He Who had spent so many years in prison without a single light at night. Imagine how the Master would love to see the millions of lights in San Francisco now![40]

Saichiro Fujita, a young Japanese, was another of the early believers who attended meetings in Helen Goodall's home in Oakland. He was employed in Kathryn Frankland's home in Fruitvale, and she had taught him about the Faith. Later, Fujita went to Wilmette to serve in the home of Mrs. Corinne True (later appointed a Hand of the Cause of God) until 'Abdu'l-Bahá sent for him to come to Haifa to serve there.[41] The Master told Fujita to grow a beard, which he did and has retained.

Fujita is a small person, very active, and he has always loved the Faith. During the war years Shoghi Effendi sent him to Japan, later recalling him to Haifa where he still serves. Fujita came to America in 1971 for a short visit, then returned to Haifa where he has a small garden of his own, which Shoghi Effendi gave him, high on Mt. Carmel. Fujita enjoys showing his garden to the pilgrims, especially to those whom he knew in California.[42]

In 1908 Helen and Ella went on pilgrimage to the Holy Land. Upon their return, they wrote a book which they titled *Daily Lessons Received at Acca*. 'Abdu'l-Bahá approved the printing of this book with these words: "You have written that upon your return you have compiled whatever you saw and heard (at Acca) and you have received the invisible assistance, that the teachings which were like invisible seeds, have sprung to life and verdancy spreading branches and leaves, and producing blossoms and fruits."[43]

Back in Oakland once again, Ella and Helen held regular weekly meetings in their Jackson Street home. Those who attended the meetings were a prayerful group, and their hearts were filled with peace and true love for each other. If one came to a meeting sad and depressed, he received comfort and his spirit was refreshed. The Cause was established on a firm foundation by those truly dedicated souls. I felt there never could be more devoted, radiant, kind, and sweet persons than Helen Goodall and Ella Cooper. Their lives and deeds were their best equipment for teaching. From the moment Helen and Ella accepted the Faith, they were active teachers.

After Ella's pilgrimage she invited me to bring to her home some of my friends to whom I had spoken of the Faith. She explained the Teachings so simply and beautifully that we became very interested and looked forward eagerly to our weekly meetings with her. Sometimes she would take us to the little tea house in her lovely garden, or, if there were just a few of us, we sat in a "cozy corner," one step up from the drawing room. She called us her "Peaches"—I suppose because we were sweet, fresh young girls; and we called her "Mother Peach," a loving name which I always used.

Ella was enthusiastic—jolly, happy, and radiant—when she taught us. She was filled with love for 'Abdu'l-Bahá, a love which she imparted to us. I remember her sparkling brown eyes as she told us stories she had heard from the Master. When the meetings were over, a delicious tea was served, which, of course, added to our enjoyment. "Moto" was always delighted at our compliments on the cheese puffs and cinnamon toast which he made for us. A spirit of loving fellowship pervaded those meetings, and we were all joyful when we parted.

Ella taught the "Peach Tree" until 1922. During those wonderful days she gave us an explanation of the Greatest Name (in Arabic *Yá Bahá'u'l-Abhá*)—"O Thou the Most Glorious of the Glorious"—which is used as an invocation to God. She shared prayers and Tablets when they came from 'Abdu'l-Bahá; she taught us the new social laws of Bahá'u'lláh and the history of the Faith. To some she gave Bahá'í ringstones, and to each she gave a little envelope containing a few flower petals which she had brought from the Shrines of the Báb and Bahá'u'lláh.

Ella told us that one day 'Abdu'l-Bahá served a melon to a guest. He saw that His guest was apparently enjoying the melon and said: "Do you not find the melon very bitter?" The guest replied: "'Abdu'l-Bahá, I have received so many sweet things from You. What does one bitter melon matter?"

Years later, when my daughter was a tiny baby, Ella would invite me to come to the meetings and bring her first "baby Peach." So I would put Barbara in a laundry basket with two handles, and one of the other "Peaches" would help me take her in the car to Ella's. To this day those of us who remain of that group are still close friends.

When the House of Worship was to be built in Wilmette, the first contribution was sent in 1912 to 'Abdu'l-Bahá from the believers in Persia. The second, also sent in 1912, was from the Oakland community, the furthermost Western community.[44] Thus Shoghi Effendi said that the House of Worship had a beginning embracing both the East and the West.[45] Friends truly sacrificed and deprived themselves to contribute to the Temple Fund, even to the extent of foregoing a meal a day for long periods of time.

Our early Feasts were held in the home of Helen Goodall and conducted according to written instructions from the Master. Usually there were about thirty friends present. Sometimes a recently returned pilgrim would give an account of his visit with 'Abdu'l-Bahá, or Helen or

Ella would read with great joy a message or a Tablet from Him. The early Feasts were not like the Feasts of today because at that time we did not have the Administrative Order. For the believers coming into the Faith today it may seem very natural that the Administrative Order is functioning vigorously. I wonder if they realize the sacrifice, effort, and time that was spent by those early believers who, at the direction of the Master, established and set in motion the administrative pattern. We had no books to study, no National Spiritual Assembly to direct us, no Guardian to guide us, no Universal House of Justice to lead us. We relied upon Tablets and instructions from our beloved 'Abdu'l-Bahá and His letters of praise for those who were firm and steadfast in working to spread the fragrances, love, and unity of His Father's Faith.

Before we gathered for Feasts each one of us prepared himself with prayers, knowing that 'Abdu'l-Bahá—our beloved Master, who carried the burden of all of the Bahá'ís on His shoulders—had said He would be present in spirit in our midst. We were met at the door by Helen and Ella, their faces illumined with beautiful smiles. We were soon seated at two long tables in the lovely dining room. There was no worldly chatter or trivial conversation. When we were seated at the table, Mrs. Goodall asked for a moment of quiet, and we silently said the Greatest Name. Then one of the believers passed from friend to friend anointing our foreheads with rose perfume and saying, "As this perfume is to the nostrils, so may this spiritual food refresh the soul." This gesture was not a ritual, but it spread the fragrance of roses throughout the room, adding sweetness, and gave us time for meditation and silent prayers. Each one then read a verse from *The Hidden Words of Bahá'u'lláh*, often followed by a prayer sent by 'Abdu'l-Bahá to Helen, which she read. After that we enjoyed the delicious material feast prepared for the guests. As we left, Helen and Ella said good-bye to us at the door and gave each of us some flowers from the tables. We left feeling closer to 'Abdu'l-Bahá and with love in our hearts for each other.

I remember that one evening Ella Bailey was chosen to anoint our foreheads with rose perfume. Ella was a school teacher in Berkeley for many years and one of the early believers who attended the meetings at Helen's home. She was truly a blessed soul with a sweet, charming, ready smile. In 1909 she received the following Tablet from 'Abdu'l-Bahá:

> To Ella M. Bailey,
> Upon her be Bahá'u'lláh!
> He is God!
> O thou maidservant of God!
> Be thou not sad on account of past vicissitudes and troubles, neither be thou discouraged by hardships and difficulties.
> Be thou hopeful in the Bounty of the True One, and be thou happy and rejoiced in the love of God.
> This world is the arena of tests, trials, and calamities. All the existing things are targets for the arrows of mortalities; therefore, one must not feel sad or disheartened on account of the travails or become hopeless over the intensity of misfortune and distress.
> Praise be to God that thou hast found the guidance of God, hast entered into the Kingdom of God, hast attained to peace and tranquility, and hast obtained a share from the Everlasting Bounty and Mercy.
> Therefore, pass the remaining days of thy life with the utmost joy and fragrance; and, with a joyful heart and tranquil mind, live and act under the protection of His Highness, the Clement.
> Upon thee be Bahá-Al-Abhá!
> ABDUL BAHA ABBAS[46]

It was Ella Bailey whom Shoghi Effendi named "the first American martyr to be laid to rest in African soil." Ella had been a cripple since childhood, never in good health, rarely free of pain. Despite her afflictions she taught the Bahá'í Faith throughout her life and made many little-known sacrifices. Ella was a living example of courage to her many friends, always happy and ready to do all she could for the Cause. She was [the first] chairman of the Berkeley Spiritual Assembly [in 1925–26].

In 1953 Ella Bailey attended the dedication of the Bahá'í House of Worship in Wilmette [and the launching of The Ten Year Crusade]. She returned to her home in the Berkeley Women's City Club, where she had always welcomed friends and inquirers. Soon after her return, in response to Shoghi Effendi's call for pioneers at that time, she arose with sublime courage to fill a post. At eighty-eight years of age, in failing health, she flew to Tripoli, Libya, to be with Robert Gulick and his family, there "to lay her bones" as she told me before she left.[47] (That expression had been used at the dedication in reference to elderly Bahá'ís who wished to pioneer.)

Ella recounted that once, during an interview with 'Abdu'l-Bahá, He had gazed a long time out of the window and then repeated her name several times, "Ella Bailey, Ella Bailey, Ella Bailey!" Then He turned to her and said, "He who loves Ella Bailey loves Me."

The first Unity Feast in the Oakland area was held at the Goodall home on March 3, 1908. The following July a Tablet was received and read by Helen in which the Master wrote of that Feast: "'Abdu'l-Bahá with His heart and soul was present at your Naw-Rúz Feast. He associated and took part in your happiness, joy, and harmonious union. Therefore, thank God that ye had such a Friend and Caller; notwithstanding the distance of the thousands of miles, He was present in spirit at your Feast of love."

All of our early Feasts in Helen's home were very spiritual. The friends showed great love for each other and made great sacrifices to attend. Those were glorious times! There was such love among the friends that we seemed to be as one, and to this day we feel a special bond.

Part 2

'Abdu'l-Bahá in California

'Abdu'l-Bahá in California

In 1908 we received the exciting news that, due to the Young Turk Revolution, the gates of the Most Great Prison [in 'Akká] had been opened and 'Abdu'l-Bahá was free. We were overjoyed. Then we learned that the Master was planning to travel to Egypt, England, France, Germany, Austria, the United States, and Canada. A letter was written and signed by us in Oakland and by some of the friends in Oregon begging Him to come to California.

When 'Abdu'l-Bahá finally arrived in America on April 11, 1912, my family sent Him a telegram of welcome. He replied from New York: "MRS. DR. ALLEN YOUR CONGRATULATING TELEGRAM CAUSES HAPPINESS MAY BLESSINGS BE UPON ALL IS MY HOPE. ABBAS." On May 1 another telegram came from Chicago: Greetings to doctor Allen, Mrs. Allen, Ramona and Warren will be here one week after which I go to Boston and Montreal then come to California. Will see you there in June God willing. Abdul Ba. Ha.

When the Master arrived in Chicago, Helen and Ella went there to greet Him. He said to them: "It makes me very happy to see you. When the hearts are pure it makes me very happy. This is what we came for—that the hearts might be made pure. I care not for ease, I care not for comfort, and when I see the pure hearts then nothing else matters."[1] When meeting the friends later in California, the Master said several times, "Your love drew Me to you."

'Abdu'l-Bahá was sixty-six years of age and in frail health when He started on His arduous travels. He made great sacrifices to spread His Father's Teachings, summoning the people of the world to promote universal peace. He had come to bless us by His presence. How little did we understand in those days the mystery of His visit.

It was October 3, 1912, when 'Abdu'l-Bahá arrived in San Francisco.[2] He had rented a lovely home at 1815 California Street, which had been selected for Him and His entourage by Helen and Ella. Shortly after He arrived there, friends started calling upon the Master. When Helen and Ella entered, He said to them: "I am tired. Therefore, I do not rise. Welcome! Last night I thought of your efforts, and I supplicated God in your behalf. May Bahá'u'lláh reward you amply, for indeed you have toiled well." As other friends arrived, 'Abdu'l-Bahá said to them: "And how are you? Welcome, very welcome! I am greatly rejoiced at meeting you all. Praise be to God you came now." Then 'Abdu'l-Bahá continued:

> Meetings are various in kind. One meeting is like the meeting of people, an ordinary meeting, which is so easily forgotten. Howsoever kind they may be to each other they will forget it. For example, a brother meeting another brother, the father meeting his son, sisters meeting, the mother meeting a daughter, or the daughter the mother, when separation takes place in the course of time gradually that relation will be forgotten. Such a meeting is without result; eventually it sinks into forgetfulness.
>
> Another meeting is similar to the meeting of the sun with the mirror. The rays of the sun shine upon the mirror. Again, there may be a meeting like the coming together of combustible wood with fire, or the mingling of oil with fire. As soon as contact is effected, combustion takes place. Ah, such a meeting is good!
>
> Again, there is a meeting which is like unto the contact of the gentle zephyrs with the trees, which exhilarates the trees, which bestows freshness and verdure; such a meeting is verily a meeting resulting in fruits and flowers.
>
> I hope that our meeting will be of this last type. May

it be like unto the meeting of the gentle zephyrs with the trees. I will supplicate that you will be fully aided in this.

A number of persons coming from the Orient to the Occident for this purpose: this is very wonderful. You cannot find a record of it in any history of any nation. At the utmost, a person, or a number of persons, may go across the continent for sightseeing, for trade or commerce, but simply to travel for the meeting of the friends and for the sake of spiritual communion, this is very rare.

This is brought about through the favors of the Blessed Perfection. This is through the bounty of Bahá'u'lláh. We witness how He has brought about this spiritual connection among the hearts and how He has attracted these hearts together.

This is one of the evidences of Bahá'u'lláh. No other except Bahá'u'lláh could bring about such a condition. No one could achieve such a colossal work, that a Persian personage and a Japanese gentleman should associate together in the utmost love here in San Francisco. This is the potency of Bahá'u'lláh.

In brief, you are very, very welcome, most welcome! You have traveled yourselves to come so far. For this I am made very happy.

I will meet you again tonight. I did not sleep last night on the train. I arrived this morning and am a little fatigued. I will meet you again soon.

On 'Abdu'l-Bahá's first day in San Francisco my mother, father, brother, and I crossed the bay on a ferryboat late in the afternoon to pay our respects to Him. When we arrived at His home, we were welcomed by friends and ushered to His room. For a moment we stood at the open door. I knew as I stood there that I expected to see an angel from Heaven. And I did! I saw the Master! He came toward us, a wonderful smile on His saintly face, extending His outstretched arms to us and saying in Persian, "Welcome! Welcome!"

That exhilarating, magic moment of seeing 'Abdu'l-

Bahá for the first time was like seeing the sun burst forth through the soft, rosy glow of dawn. It brought the nearness of God, and my heart was filled with praise and gratitude for the bounty of being with Him. I knew that His visit to California was a very special gift from God. As we entered the presence of the Master, He appeared to be enveloped in a beautiful, ethereal, luminous light. The room seemed flooded with sunshine. Flowers were everywhere, and their fragrance filled the air. As 'Abdu'l-Bahá stood there in His native dress, an 'abá and turban, He was surrounded by a golden glow. My heart felt as though it would burst with joy and happiness to be at last in the presence of the beloved Master, to see Him with my own eyes and hear His beautiful voice as He spoke to my precious family.

The Master took my mother's hands and said, "Welcome, Mrs. Allen, welcome, very welcome! You have a very united family, a very united family, and you will all be united through all the worlds of God." His words to my mother made us very happy. Then in His warm, gentle hands He took the hand of each one of us and welcomed us. When I gave 'Abdu'l-Bahá some yellow roses I had gathered from our garden, He was very pleased. He smiled as He thanked me and seemed happy with my small gift, for He knew that my love went with it. As He looked into my eyes, His gentle, smiling eyes touched my soul; they seemed to tell me that He knew what was in my heart and everything about me. I felt as though I were in another world. At that moment I silently gave my heart and dedicated my life to Him.

He invited us to be seated, and continued speaking, telling us how happy He was to meet the California believers and that He hoped His Father's Message would reach the hearts of the people. He conversed with us as though we were old friends, and to each of us He spoke some special words. Then 'Abdu'l-Bahá arose from His chair and, stepping lightly, but like a king, served us with His own hands, in small crystal glasses, the most delicious tea I had ever tasted. It was light amber-colored Persian tea which He had brought with Him. To this day I can remember its fragrance and taste its sweetness.

The happiness of that first meeting has remained with me all of my life. We knew that we were blessed and privileged to be in the presence of 'Abdu'l-Bahá. We were full of deep joy as we basked in His love. Soon it was time to take our leave, for other people were waiting to greet Him.

Friends have asked me to describe 'Abdu'l-Bahá. How can anyone describe Him? Each one of us saw Him with our own spiritual and physical eyes. It seemed that in Him we found what we most longed for. In the Master's presence I felt as though I were in another world. In those moments I seemed most conscious of His overpowering love for all mankind. From childhood 'Abdu'l-Bahá had been endowed with physical beauty, we are told. Despite His advanced age and the vicissitudes He had endured, His carriage was majestic and His posture remarkable. He seemed to me to be about five feet, nine inches tall, although His long 'abá and His white turban may have caused Him to appear taller than He was. He was strong and vibrant. He walked lightly, so that there were moments when He seemed hardly to touch the ground.

'Abdu'l-Bahá enjoyed walking. His secretaries usually accompanied Him. On the street people would turn and glance at Him, and many curious eyes followed Him as He strolled along with great dignity and grace in His Eastern robe and turban. 'Abdu'l-Bahá always wore His native dress, which was a full-length, light-colored robe, over which He wore an 'abá, or cloak, of beige, tan, brown, or cream color. His shoes were of soft brown leather, partly covering the instep and heel. He wore a low turban wound around with folds of soft white material from under which His wispy silver hair fell to His shoulders. Encircling His often-smiling lips was a white mustache and a short, rounded beard. The Master had well-defined, slightly bushy, white eyebrows. To the astonishment of each person who talked with Him, His eyes seemed to change color as He spoke. Sometimes they looked blue or hazel or grey, with a tiny white line encircling the iris. On the day He spoke to the "Peach Tree" His eyes were very blue, and they sparkled. Once, when 'Abdu'l-Bahá spoke of the terrible treatment and exile of Bahá'u'lláh, His eyes looked black and shiny.

When the Master's face was in repose, deep lines often appeared on His cheeks and between His brows, and His eyes looked sad and showed the suffering He had endured. However, when 'Abdu'l-Bahá smiled, the sadness vanished, and one saw only glorious beauty in His face, especially when He spoke of His Father's principles. The Master's complexion was a warm, light tan. His hands were square, strong, yet delicate; when He held your hand, His clasp felt warm and friendly.

As with His eyes so did 'Abdu'l-Bahá's voice change when He spoke on different subjects. At times it was soft and gentle, low and penetrating; or it was loud and firm. His language was always exquisite. His pleasing, musical tones touched our hearts as He chanted a prayer. Despite the Master's fatigue at times, and His physical ailments, He welcomed everyone with a beaming smile, and in His pleasing and vibrant voice would ask, "Are you happy?"

He loved the sound of laughter and often told stories and anecdotes to make us laugh. When we heard Him laugh, we knew that He or someone else had told an amusing story, and the sound of His laughter made us all happy. Once the Master told us that during the most dangerous and trying times of His imprisonment Bahá'u'lláh would ask each member of the family to relate the most amusing incident or story they had experienced or heard that day. After the tale had been told, they would all roar with laughter.

Later on the day of 'Abdu'l-Bahá's arrival we went to the home of Helen Goodall in Oakland to be again in His presence. When the friends were gathered, He said to them:

> In the world many people go from one country to another. . . . such journeys are for travel, or commer-

cial purposes, or for some political reason, or the motive may be some scientific achievement, or they go on journies [sic] in order to meet friends. All such meetings are accidental; they are concerned with the exigencies of the world of nature.

But I have come from the Orient to the Occident—this vast distance have I crossed with no commercial purpose in view, nor travel as an object, nor politics as a reason. It has been simply to meet you. . . . our meeting is real, essential—for the hearts are connected and the souls are attracted and the spirits are exhilarated, and such a meeting is *real* in character, and great are the results therefrom. The results are everlasting.

. . . .

Praise be to God! We have assembled here, and the cause of our gathering here is the love of God. . . .

I am hopeful that the hearts may be moved, the souls may be attracted, and that all will act in accordance with the teachings of BAHA'O'LLAH.[3]

That evening, when more of the friends had come to be with Him, the Master said: "I am going to say, 'Welcome,' to you, instead of your welcoming me. I am most happy to be here with you. I am exceedingly joyous, and I offered thanks to His Holiness BAHA'O'LLAH that the potency of His Word was instrumental in bringing about such a meeting."[4]

Summoning superhuman strength, courage, and resolution, the Master sacrificed Himself to spread the Teachings of Bahá'u'lláh. Before He made this trip, He had never given a public speech or addressed audiences made up of both men and women. Yet He accustomed Himself to the ways and manners of the Western world. 'Abdu'l-Bahá spoke with great eloquence, wisdom, and brilliance. He spoke in simple language to professors, teachers, clergy, youth, and people in all walks of life. He seemed to have a mysterious power to win the love and respect of all. The Master spoke with such authority and explained profound subjects in such a clear and simple way, that often no one questioned what He said. He always spoke in a kindly, loving manner. At times 'Abdu'l-Bahá was seated as He spoke. At other times He would walk back and forth or stand quietly. He seemed always to be surrounded by a lovely, celestial radiance.

During the three weeks that the Master stayed in California, He traveled to many places: Oakland, Berkeley, Palo Alto, Los Angeles, Pasadena, and Sacramento. 'Abdu'l-Bahá's visit caused a great deal of publicity. In an interview by a reporter from the San Francisco *Examiner*, 'Abdu'l-Bahá was asked, "What is your object in coming to America?" He replied, "I have come to America to promote the ideal of Universal Peace and the solidarity of the human race. I have not come for pleasure or as a tourist."[5]

'Abdu'l-Bahá was invited to speak at many places. He spoke at colleges, in churches, at the School for the Blind in Oakland, and to the Peace Society and the Theosophical Society in the Bay Area. At the invitation of Mayor Stitt Wilson of Berkeley, the Master gave His only public address in that city [on October 9] at the Berkeley High School, where He was received with great reverence and respect. The auditorium was filled to capacity. On another occasion 'Abdu'l-Bahá spoke to the Berkeley Short Story Club, of which my mother was a member. Several members of the club had attended my mother's Bahá'í meetings and were pleased and appreciative that the Master had agreed to address the club.

The Master often spoke at three or four meetings in one day. We were amazed at His ceaseless activity. Whenever He spoke, He gave to the audience what they most needed to hear and what would help them. He satisfied each listener's spiritual longing with His love. The overpowering conviction in His words made a deep impression upon His listeners.

While He was in California, many of 'Abdu'l-Bahá's activities were arranged by Helen and Ella. It was an exciting evening when He spoke in the [First] Congregational Church in Oakland on October 6. The church was

'ABDU'L-BAHÁ
shown surrounded by children and their parents
he steps of the home of Helen Goodall in Oakland, California,
after His meeting with the children on October 12, 1912.

'ABDU'L-BAHÁ
standing in the quadrangle in front of the M
of Leland Stanford Junior University, Palo A
where He spoke on October 8, 1

THE ALLEN FAMILY
Back row, left to right: Frances Orr Allen, Dr. Woodson Allen.
Front row, left to right: Ramona Allen, Joseph Bray, Gertrude Mitchell (Allen), Warren Allen.

Lloyd Lake in Golden Gate Park in San Francisco
where 'Abdu'l-Bahá would leave the automobile
and walk along the shore,
then stand and watch the ducks swim toward Him.
In the background is the marble arch,
called "Portals of the Past,"
from the Towne family mansion.
The author is shown visiting
the spot in 1965.

crowded. I sat in the balcony above the pulpit where the Master stood. All at once I realized that He was very fatigued. Instead of listening I began to say a healing prayer for Him. Suddenly, 'Abdu'l-Bahá seemed to grow in stature and become strong, and His voice grew loud and clear. I knew that He had, before our eyes, drawn on the "'Power of the Great Ether.'"[6] He gave a brilliant talk and later met with the friends, appearing quite rejuvenated.

On October 7 'Abdu'l-Bahá spoke in Oakland to a Japanese audience of the [Japanese] Young Men's Christian Association. On the 8th He went to Palo Alto where He spoke at Leland Stanford Junior University. That memorable morning a group of us from Oakland and Berkeley eagerly went by train to Palo Alto. From there we went to the Stanford Memorial Chapel, where we were seated among nearly fifteen hundred people, including students, faculty members, and guests.[7] The audience listened with quiet esteem and admiration as the Master spoke about the oneness of all phenomena. After He had finished speaking, the President of the University, David Starr Jordan, closed the program by saying: "We are all under very great obligation to Abdul Baha for this illuminating expression of the brotherhood of man and the value of international peace. I think we can best show our appreciation by simply a rising vote of thanks."[8]

After the meeting we all went outside of the Chapel. There I saw the Master standing alone in the quadrangle. Hesitatingly I approached Him and asked permission to take His photograph. Courteously He granted me the privilege; and I took a picture showing 'Abdu'l-Bahá with the Stanford Chapel in the background.

That day Dr. Ernest Rogers, a Bahá'í who was head of the Montezuma Mountain School for Boys near Los Gatos, took about thirty students to hear the Master speak. Los Gatos was thirty miles south of Palo Alto, and the boys had to walk five miles each way en route between the train and the university.

Professor Rogers had been a Bahá'í for a long time,

having first heard about the Faith in a letter which Mrs. Brittingham wrote to his mother. In 1900 he had received this Tablet from 'Abdu'l-Bahá:

> To Mr. Ernest A. Rogers:
> O thou who art advancing toward God!
> Verily, I am informed of the text of thy letter, which contained how thou art confessing the Kingdom of God and art attracted by the Love of Bahá, in those regions.
> Thank God, for that He hath made thee of the "Chosen Ones," not of those who were only "called"; hath assigned thee to the knowledge of His Manifest Beauty, during the Great Century; hath guided thee to the right Way; hath exhilarated thee from the Cup which is overflowing with the choice Wine of the Love of God; hath dilated thy breast with the light of knowledge of God; hath favored thee with His Gifts; and hath attracted thee from this world through the Magnet of the Kingdom. Therefore, speak eloquently the praise of God, for this Greatest Gift and excellent favor.
> May Greetings and praise be upon thee!
> 'Abdu'l-Bahá 'Abbás[9]

After the talk [at Stanford] 'Abdu'l-Bahá was the guest of President Jordan with whom He drove in the afternoon. Later He visited the home of Mrs. I. C. Merriman in Palo Alto. That evening the Master spoke on the "Reality of Divinity" at the [Palo Altan] Unitarian Church. Reverend Clarence Reed, pastor of the church, said at the close of the Master's discourse: "I feel that a man of God has spoken to us tonight. I know no better way to close the service than with a prayer; not a prayer in spoken words, but a prayer in silence. Let each person pray in his own way for the coming of the universal religion, the religion of love, the religion of peace—a religion of the fullness of life." After a moment of silence everyone departed.[10] 'Abdu'l-Bahá and His entourage remained one night as the guests of Mrs. Merriman's daughter and the next day returned to San Francisco.

During the Master's stay in San Francisco some of the friends would be at His home in the kitchen preparing special dishes for Him ('Abdu'l-Bahá was especially fond of different kinds of broth); other friends would do anything they could to make Him happy and His stay pleasant. People would flock to His home from early morning until late at night, bringing gifts of fruit, candy, and other things which the Master would promptly share with everyone. Once He said, "Take these flowers downstairs so that all the friends will see them. I will enjoy them there." During an interview my mother had with 'Abdu'l-Bahá He gave her a pomegranate to eat and flowers; after her death I found the pressed flowers and the skin of the pomegranate among her treasures.

Although I lived in Berkeley, I spent every moment I could in the Master's house in San Francisco, sitting with the friends in the hall or in the living room, hoping to see Him pass and look upon His blessed and radiant face or hear His wonderful voice as He greeted the many friends, often speaking to someone in particular. One morning I was sitting quietly in a room by myself, awaiting the thrilling moment when I would see 'Abdu'l-Bahá pass by the open door. Just then I had a sudden awakening. I asked myself what magic 'Abdu'l-Bahá possessed that drew my love to Him and made me happy just to be in the same place where He was. I reflected how each time I was in His presence I longed to draw from Him some of His spiritual radiance, and I prayed that I might acquire virtues and reflect in my life His beautiful Teachings. I realized that the ability to reflect these spiritual qualities could not be a gift, but that I must earn that bounty through deeds, prayer, effort, and study of the Holy Words.

'Abdu'l-Bahá possessed a power that made me long to be an exemplary Bahá'í. Each time I was in the presence of the Master, He awakened in my heart a new kind of love for all people. His every word was an inspiration to me to be a better Bahá'í. He treated each person very specially, and He showered His love over all of the friends. No one could resist His radiant happiness. To hear 'Abdu'l-Bahá say, "Are you happy? Are you happy?" filled our day with joy. He lived the perfect Bahá'í life. He inspired each soul to follow in His path. This was His magic.

Every day the atmosphere was filled with thrilling excitement, and everyone was happy just to be in the Master's home. Everything seemed to be suspended during those precious days, and often I lost all sense of time. When I could, I went wherever 'Abdu'l-Bahá was to speak because I did not want to miss being in His presence or hearing His words and exhortations to the friends and the people.

Believers were constantly arriving from Portland, Seattle, Sacramento, Los Angeles, and other cities; and each one had some moments with Him. Harriett and James Latimer, my aunt and uncle, and their son, George, came from Portland, Oregon, and remained in San Francisco during the Master's stay there. He gave my aunt the name *Ruhaniyyih* and called her the "Mother of the Portland Assembly" (Community), as the Latimer family had established the Faith in that city. George traveled around the world teaching and fulfilling the wishes of the Master. He made two pilgrimages to Haifa to meet 'Abdu'l-Bahá and several pilgrimages to meet Shoghi Effendi. George served on the National Spiritual Assembly of the United States for many years until his death in June 1948.[11]

Soon after George's passing, my aunt received this letter from the National Spiritual Assembly:

November 16, 1948

Dear Ruhaniyyih:

Now we can see and recognize the extraordinary spiritual unity of the great Bahá'í services rendered by you, your husband and your son. Such work could never have been done by any three individuals striving alone. It could only be a family accomplishment, a unity—one inspiration flowing through three harmonious instruments. . . .

With loving greetings from each member,
> Affectionately yours,
> Horace Holley
> Secretary

'Abdu'l-Bahá provided the inspiration for such unity. Whenever we were in His presence, He made us feel secure and assured of His love for us. He showed such love that, if one were sad, He gently made him happy. The Master always spread good cheer. One of the friends was not able to hold back her tears in His presence. He said to her, "Weep on. Beyond the tears is sunshine." In those days we all felt united in our devoted love for Him. 'Abdu'l-Bahá often told us, "Love is the greatest of all living powers."

It was a joyous time for all of us. The friends from near and far gathered in the home of 'Abdu'l-Bahá, hoping to have a word with Him or just to see Him pass through the rooms and hallways, saying in Persian, *"Marhabá! Marhabá!"* (Welcome! Welcome!). One day, while I was sitting in the hall, I heard my name called. When I responded, I learned that the Master had invited me to have lunch with Him. My heart leaped with joy, and I was so excited that I could scarcely move.

'Abdu'l-Bahá stood at the door of the dining room with a loving, tender smile of welcome on His happy face as I entered. He seated Mrs. Anna Monroe to His right and me next to her. He urged us to eat and enjoy our lunch, telling amusing stories to make us laugh. At one point, to my surprise, He reached for a slice of bread, broke off a large piece, and put it on Mrs. Monroe's plate. Then He put a tiny portion on my plate. He looked at me and laughed, and so did I as I ate my tiny portion. Mrs. Monroe did not touch her piece of bread. We know that every word and act of 'Abdu'l-Bahá's had a special meaning. I remember that Mrs. Monroe [who introduced us to the Faith] did not remain interested in it during the last years of her life.

Later, the Master reached for a bunch of grapes and dropped them into my glass of water. I looked at them, and He laughed as He saw that I was puzzled as to what to do. I felt it would be rude to put my hand into the glass to take them out, but I ate two grapes which hung over the rim of the glass and sadly left the rest. During the luncheon 'Abdu'l-Bahá would lean over, look at me, and laugh; and so did I. He conversed with others at the table, but I was too overwhelmed to remember what was said.

The Master was fond of Edam cheese, and there was a large cheese on the table in front of Him. He also enjoyed California cucumbers; during the luncheon He took one and, holding it in His left hand, peeled it down a little, sliced it very thin, and ate it. (In Haifa cucumbers grow smaller, are very juicy, and are enjoyed as a fruit.) 'Abdu'l-Bahá told a funny story, and we all laughed. Then we parted. I wanted very much to return to the dining room and get that bunch of grapes, but regretfully I did not go back.

On October 10 in San Francisco 'Abdu'l-Bahá went to visit Charles Tinsley, a black Bahá'í who had been laid up for a long time with a broken leg. "I am impatient," said Mr. Tinsley, "to be up and out to work for the Cause."

The Master told him:

> You must not be sad. This affliction will make you spiritually stronger. . . . you are dear to me. I will tell you a story:—
>
> A certain ruler wished to appoint one of his subjects to a high office; so, in order to train him, the ruler cast him into prison and caused him to suffer much. The man was surprised at this, for he expected great favors. The ruler had him taken from prison and beaten with sticks. This greatly astonished the man, for he thought the ruler loved him. After this he was hanged on the gallows until he was nearly dead. After he recovered he asked the ruler, "If you love me, why did you do these things?" The ruler replied: "I wish to make you prime minister. By having gone through these ordeals you are better fitted for that office. I wish you to know how it is yourself. When you are obliged to punish, you will

know how it feels to endure these things. I love you so I wish you to become perfect.

'Abdu'l-Bahá then said to Charles:

> Even so with you. After this ordeal you will reach maturity. God sometimes causes us to suffer much and to have many misfortunes that we may become strong in His Cause.
>
> You will soon recover and be spiritually stronger than ever before. You will work for God and carry the Message to many of your people.[12]

After this visit, the Master told Helen Goodall and Dr. Woodson Allen, with whom He was riding in an automobile, "Nothing makes a man so happy as love." He continued:

> There will come a day when you will see how the nightingales of Persia will sing their songs of God in these gardens. Likewise, the quails of America in the mountains of Persia shall cause such a "quailing" as to cause the mountains to dance. The East and the West will then have a feast, and in one direction the song of the nightingale will be heard, and in the other direction you will hear the songs of other birds. In one direction you will hear the music of God, and from another region you will find the outpouring of God's blessings. In one direction you will see the lights of the radiance of guidance; in the other direction the Sun of Reality will shine. In another you will find the Chalice of the Love of God passed around. In the world there will be a spiritual feast. From the beginning of the world to the present day there will be none similar; hearts will be rejoiced, spirits will be exhilarated. The world will become a paradise of Abha.

When the Master was in the city Mrs. Goodall would drive Him and some of the friends (often including my father) to Lloyd Lake, a small lake surrounded by trees and flowering shrubs, in Golden Gate Park. On the edge of the lake was placed a marble arch, which is all that remains of the Towne family mansion after the fire of 1906. This arch is called "Portals of the Past" and is on the shore across the lake from where the Master would stand on the path and watch the ducks. The little ducks swam toward Him as if drawn by His presence. Once He said, "The ducks and flowers are more conscious of My presence than are the people of the city." He spoke of many things and said that He hoped the Faith would progress in the West.

On one of His visits to Golden Gate Park with a few friends 'Abdu'l-Bahá spoke to my father about health:

> ['Abdu'l-Bahá]: Man must not imagine disease but must ever trust God. Anyway, a man's life here in this world is temporary. He is in a world that is like a house, susceptible to every invasion, and God must protect man—man must be submissive to God. He must not occupy himself with the thoughts of things—imaginings. If a man thinks too much of his health, he will become afflicted. . . .
>
> The spiritual life of man is important. The everlasting life of man is of the utmost importance. A man must be thinking of that. . . .
>
> Dr. Allen: Why should we pay attention to the everlasting life? We give up all of our time to this, and why should we be thinking about the rest of it?
>
> Mrs. [Lua] Getsinger: You mean why should we not wait until we get there and take it up then?
>
> 'Abdu'l-Bahá: Because whatsoever a man soweth here he reapeth there. This world is like a school. He must learn lessons here so that when he issues from this school he may become learned. He must not be ignorant.
>
> For phenomena in general, there is one virtue. It is innate virtue. For example, this tree: its verdure is innate; its flowers are innate; they are creational. It does not interfere with them. It has no will of its own.

As to animals, all their virtues are innate. The sun, its virtues are innate; therefore, there is no credit to be given it. . . . Are you grateful to any of these? Not especially, as they are innate, involuntary virtues. But the virtues of man are acquired. . . . Therefore, for man there is need of the acquiring of virtues.

All the philosophers have come with the intention of teaching man to acquire virtues. All the prophets who have come have come to endow man with acquired virtues. . . .

When the party returned from the park to 'Abdu'l-Bahá's home, He continued:

I have traversed long distances to see you. Bahá'ís traverse long distances to see one another. His Holiness Bahá'u'lláh says: "My comfort, My ease, My life, My honor, My faith, My family, My household, all have I sacrificed in order that blessed souls may appear, souls that might be centers of the virtues of mankind. May they be the souls of the Kingdom, so heavenly, so lordly, and freed from the attachments of the nether world, sanctified from all the vices of human nature, acquiring beauties from the perfections of God." Thus He endured every difficulty. All these ordeals He suffered, and He sacrificed Himself for all of us.

On October 12, 1912, 'Abdu'l-Bahá was invited by Rabbi Martin A. Meyer to speak at Temple Emmanu-El in San Francisco. Time has not dimmed my memory of the Master as He stood in the temple between two lovely palm trees while a shaft of light from a window fell across Him and bathed Him in the morning sunshine. There were two thousand Jews present as 'Abdu'l-Bahá spoke about "The Fundamental Unity of Religious Thought." Listening to the words of the Master, I realized that in that vast temple there was absolute silence except for His pleasing, vibrant voice calling all to unity and urging the congregation to respect the names of Jesus and Muḥammad and above all to be kind to all mankind. He gave proof of Jesus' claim and asked the people to set aside all religious prejudice. In closing He said:

> The age has dawned when human fellowship will become a reality.
> The century has come when all religions shall be unified.
> The dispensation is at hand when all nations shall enjoy the blessings of International Peace. . . .
> For all mankind shall dwell in peace and security beneath the shelter of the great tabernacle of the one living God.[13]

Later that Saturday afternoon, October 12, Helen and Ella held a party at their Oakland home for the children to meet 'Abdu'l-Bahá. It was a lovely and amusing sight to see the little ones rush to Him. The Master would take them in His arms, kiss them, and hold them on His lap. He gave them candy and flowers. To each of us He gave an envelope containing rose petals from the Holy Shrines. The children welcomed 'Abdu'l-Bahá by singing "Softly His Voice Is Calling Now." Then the Master spoke to the children:

> What radiant children these are! How radiant! What radiant and beautiful children!
> These will become very good, because they will receive Bahá'í education. They will be reared beneath the shelter of Bahá'u'lláh. They are just like fresh plants which have been sown in the Garden of Abhá. They will be reared through the heat of the Sun of Reality. Assuredly, amongst them will appear souls—most blessed souls—each one of whom will be a radiant candle in the world of humanity, souls who will shine from the Eternal Horizon even as stars shine.
> They are very, very (charming) indeed—exceedingly (charming). A tree is different in its various states of development, such as when it is nigh unto fruitage, when it comes under the education of the gardener, when a fresh plant, from the very beginning is to be

reared and cultured by a skilled gardener, because the latter—the fresh plant—can be educated according to the wishes of the gardener, and the gardener can train each branch just as he wishes it to grow.

Now, these children are fresh plants which have fallen into the hands of the gardener. Therefore, they will be very well educated; they will become fruitful trees; they will become very blessed trees; they will become most delectable trees. The Gardener is blessed, and the skill of the Gardener will become manifest in them.

A beautiful photograph was taken of 'Abdu'l-Bahá, the children, and the friends at the time of this party.

On another joyous occasion in San Francisco the Master again addressed the children:

> You are all my grandchildren.
>
> I feel the utmost joy to be present here with you, especially to be surrounded with such radiant children. They are the very flowers of the Paradise of Abhá.
>
> Surely, a man in a rose garden is to be happy, and now I am in a rose garden. On one side, trees most fruitful and delightful do I see, and, on the other hand, I see my children who are flowers and most delightful to look at, and, assuredly, that gives joy in such a place.
>
> In San Francisco, through the hand of the Gardener of God, who has appeared in the Orient, to see such a garden as the result of His handiwork in the West—this is a source of great thanksgiving in the East. Hence I am hopeful, through the favors of that Real Gardener, that He may ever care for these trees, and water them; that He may ever refresh, through His Holy Dewdrops, His flowers; may shower upon them from His clouds of Mercy. May the Sun of His Reality shine upon them all. May they bask in the sunshine of His praises. May, day by day, this garden become more green and verdant, its trees become mightier and more beautiful, its flowers become more delicate and fresh, in order that the delightful fragrance of this garden shall refresh the

nostrils of the longing ones, both in the East and the West.

An Oriental personage, having come from the most remote part of the Orient, were he to inhale the fragrances which are wafting from the distant parts of the West, he would say: "How fragrant are they! Evidently the rose garden of the West is most beautiful. Its flowers blossomed delightfully. The fragrance thereof is reaching even this remote district, and may this cause the rose garden of the East to be proud of this, that, praise be to God, the rose garden of the West, in a short space of time, has assumed most delightful freshness. Most magnificent flowers have become apparent therein. Variegated flowers can be seen there. White flowers have grown in it; colored flowers have grown in it; red flowers can be seen in it; and yellow flowers can be seen in it, and all of these together are in the utmost of freshness and verdure, and each lends a charm and harmony to the others. Each one is a cause of adornment to the others.

This is my hope, and so do I wish through the favors of Bahá'u'lláh, may He bless these children.

[Going to each child separately] May He bless this child.

'Abdu'l-Bahá never let a heart be hurt, and He never left anyone without making him happy. He was always extremely courteous to everyone. Shortly before the Master's departure my mother, with the Master's consent, invited a group of friends to meet Him in her home in Berkeley. Time passed, but 'Abdu'l-Bahá did not appear, and she and her guests were greatly disappointed. Later we learned that a believer had driven Him to the California redwoods and failed to return in time for the meeting. Afterward the following message, dated December 2, 1912, was received by Ella Cooper from the Master: "Convey most wonderful greetings of Abhá to the maidservant of God Mrs. Allen, and show unto her the utmost kindness on My behalf. Although in body I did not go to her house, yet in spirit and soul I was present in her assemblage."¹⁴

There were times when 'Abdu'l-Bahá disciplined the friends, but always with love and mercy. He gave to each one what was best for him, as well as often what they most wished for. His daily life was an example of His Teachings to all of us. Surely He knew how much we longed to be like Him, even to the slightest degree.

'Abdu'l-Bahá spent three days in the country at the home of Phoebe Hearst in Pleasanton. Phoebe arrived at the Master's home [on October 14], to escort Him there. Before they drove off in a big black limousine, the chauffeur drew the shades down, I suppose to protect 'Abdu'l-Bahá from the public's gaze. We stood on the sidewalk and watched as the car pulled away. We felt lonesome, and it seemed that the sunshine had left us. I was told later that, upon the Master's departure from the Hacienda, He gave Phoebe a most precious and priceless Persian rug.

Arriving back from Pleasanton on October 16, 'Abdu'l-Bahá spoke to friends from Portland who were gathered in His home:

> Alláh-u-Abhá! You are very welcome. Be seated. You are very, very welcome! Because I longed to see you, I have shortened my visit to the country, and here am I. All be seated. I longed very much to see you all and (to the children) to see you and to kiss you. At Pleasanton the air was very good, very pleasant, elevated and beautiful surroundings. The views are delightful. Are you all well?
>
> May you always be happy. All My endeavors are for the purpose that you may be happy. Praise be to God you are beneath the shelter of Bahá'u'lláh. Praise be to God the doors of the Kingdom are open for you. Praise be to God the Light of the Sun of Reality is shining upon you.
>
> Praise be to God heavenly manna is descending for you, and if you be not happy who is to be happy? If you

be not attracted, who is to be attracted? If you be not thankful, who is to be thankful? If you appreciated the Great Bestowal, you would surely fly—absolutely fly; out of excessive joy, you would soar. For that which was the greatest desire of the Saints you have attained to without any trouble (laughing), without any trials, without any ordeals, without any difficulties—out of absolute mercy.

In the late afternoon of October 16 the Master was host for a wonderful Feast at Helen Goodall's home in Oakland. There were one hundred and twenty present from California, Oregon, and Washington.[15] There were Dutch, French, Swiss, Persian, English, Japanese, and Canadian friends. A young Hindu attended, and 'Abdu'l-Bahá said of him, "This Hindu son is a son of Mine."

The three large rooms—the drawing room, the library, and the dining room—and the spacious entrance hall held long tables where the friends sat. The tables were decorated with yellow and gold chrysanthemums and fall-colored flowers. Large bowls filled with luscious fruits, candies, and cakes were in abundance. When we were all seated, the Master invited us to partake of the delicious food that was served. He stood between the spacious hall and the drawing room so that all of the friends could hear Him, and He said:

> Praise be to God! you are the guests of Mrs. Goodall. With the utmost love has she prepared this feast, and every kind of food is before you. . . .
> This is a heavenly feast, an excellent meeting. . . . The Supreme Concourse is now beholding this assemblage, proclaiming aloud: *"Blessed are ye! Blessed are ye! Blessed are ye who are the servants of* BAHA'O'LLAH! *Blessed are ye who are the manifestors of faith! Blessed are ye who have such radiant countenances! Blessed are ye whose hearts are like unto rose gardens.*[16]

We were blessed, He told us, for we had the bounty of His

presence commemorating Bahá'u'lláh among us.

'Abdu'l-Bahá strolled from room to room, pausing now and then to take a piece of fruit or a sweet and put it on someone's plate. I was seated next to Madame Khan. I remember that He placed candy on our plates. She took hers and, as is the custom in Persia when one receives a precious gift, raised it to her heart, her lips, and her forehead before eating it. When He passed by or paused near us, we stopped eating; but He asked us to continue enjoying the bountiful repast while He talked.

As the Master walked through the rooms, He spoke of His Father's Revelation, telling us how we could become followers in His path. The rooms seemed filled with His radiance, and His smile included us all. The feeling of happiness was almost overpowering! Each one felt His love pouring over us.

> Praise be to God! you are imbued with spiritual susceptibilities, for verily you have been gathered together in this meeting through the love of God. It is the bounty of the Kingdom which has summoned you here. It is the Most Great Guidance which has called you here. It is the power of attraction which has drawn you together here, and it is the bestowal of the Kingdom of ABHA which has invited you to this feast. These are spiritual susceptibilities, and these are emanations of the conscience. Because of these susceptibilities, this radiant youth is seated here, and in the utmost of love I am patting him on the shoulder.[17]

The young man 'Abdu'l-Bahá mentioned was Mr. Robinson, the husband of Ella's cousin Alice Robinson. I wondered why 'Abdu'l-Bahá had chosen this young man for such a blessing.

Later Mr. John W. Matteson, who was seated with me at the same table, told me this story. Those were days of spiritual investigation for many of the friends, and Mr. and Mrs. Matteson were searching for truth. When he saw the Master put His hands on that young man's shoulder,

Mr. Matteson thought to himself, "If 'Abdu'l-Bahá did that same thing to me, I would believe." However, the Master strolled into the other rooms. Presently He returned to that room, walked straight to Mr. Matteson, and placed His hands upon the young man's shoulders. From that moment Mr. Matteson became, until his death in 1958, one of the most faithful followers of Bahá'u'lláh. He and his wife, Berdette, served in outstanding ways, and their son and daughter-in-law, Lorne and Eleanor, and their sons, are all ardent and active Bahá'ís in the Bay Area. Berdette Matteson passed away in Hayward, California, in January 1971.

The Feast was almost over when suddenly 'Abdu'l-Bahá started up the stairway leading from the hall. There was a hush as we watched Him go, and we thought that He was leaving us. The Master stopped on a small balcony, halfway to the second floor, in front of a beautiful stained glass window. Then He stepped forward and, extending His arms with palms upturned, chanted this beautiful benediction:

> O kind Lord, verily this assemblage is longing for Thee and loving Thy beauty. Verily, these friends are set aglow with the fire of Thy love and are joyful because of Thy presence. They have turned to Thy Kingdom, seeking naught but Thy good pleasure, desiring naught but to pursue Thy pathway, and seeking naught save Thy good will. Not a day passes but they are occupied with Thy commemoration and are ever ready to serve Thee.
>
> O God, illumine these hearts. O God, make joyous these lives. O Lord, suffer these souls to attain to the superlative degree of spirituality in the world of humanity. O Lord, suffer these souls to become truly distinguished, and make them the manifestors of Thy favor and the recipients of Thy good gifts. Shine upon them with Thy radiant splendor, waft over them the breeze of Thy providence, and pour upon them the rain of bestowals from the clouds of Thy generosity. Thus these souls, like the flowers of the rose garden, shall grow in

verdure and freshness, and among all mankind shall they be redolent of delightful fragrance.

O Lord, confirm them all in Thy service, and aid them in guiding others to Thee. Brighten the eyes through witnessing Thy great signs; fill the ears with harmonies through Thy melodies; and refresh the nostrils through the fragrances of Thy Kingdom. Confer upon these souls the life everlasting, gathering them all together beneath the tabernacle of the oneness of the world of humanity.

Verily, Thou art the Almighty! Verily, Thou art the Powerful! Verily, Thou art the Giver of good gifts.[18]

The Master continued up the stairs. Soon we all departed with hearts and minds filled with the wonder of 'Abdu'l-Bahá.

I was present at the Master's house on the afternoon of October 17 when He addressed a group of the friends, including those from Seattle, Portland, and Spokane:

> You are all welcome, very welcome. The friends from Seattle and Portland have labored very much to have come such a long distance here (laughing). I am very much ashamed because it was my part to go there and see them. But what could I have done? I did not have the time.
>
> The purpose was to have a visit, to meet. Praise be to God, that is obtained. Whether I go there or you come here, the end is meeting. God has brought the hearts there together. Although the bodies are distant and far apart, the spirits are very near. Though we may be in the Orient and you in the Occident, praise be to God the hearts are connected, the spirits are near to each other, the consciences are inclined toward each other. The hearts are attracted.
>
> We are all the waves of one sea. We are all the flowers of one garden. We are all the trees of one mountain. We are together. We are associating. We are affiliating in the utmost of happiness.
>
> If two or more people in one country, one city, and of

one race, associate with each other, it is not astonishing. They have not accomplished a great thing. It is a natural thing.

Amongst the animals this sort of fellowship exists. The animals which live in the same pasture, they exercise fellowship toward each other.

This, however, is astonishing, that souls from the Orient and souls from the Occident should be in the utmost of love and fellowship. Doves from Asia, from America, from Europe, from India and from Japan—if these should flock together, associate with each other, fly together, enjoy themselves, and pick up grains together, this is very good. This is astonishing. How did these come together?

Some philosophers, who were among the divine philosophers, were capable of causing fellowship to exist among a certain number of people, although the fellowship was outward and temporary; but they were unable to establish universal education, but the Holy Divine Manifestations of God accomplished universal education. They united the East and the West. They improved the morals of man. They changed the thoughts of man. They transformed the conduct of man. This is not possible through human power. This is possible through the dominion of the Kingdom. It is possible through the Breath of the Holy Spirit.

Therefore, thank God that you are confirmed in this Cause and that you will be instrumental in bringing about the existence of amity and love amongst all humanity.

Cathryn O'Reilly, my cousin from Portland, had brought the Master a large bouquet of white roses. He said to her: "This is a good gift. White is very good, excellent. Thank you!" Then 'Abdu'l-Bahá wrote on a photograph of Himself for her: "O Thou kind God! Confer shelter to this maidservant of Thine in the neighborhood of Thy most Great Bestowal."

Cathryn asked: "Have I any special work? I have no home. . . ." The Master replied: "What do you want? A placeless person is better off. . . . The whole world belongs to you. A placeless man has the whole world. A nestless bird is sheltered by every tree and can rest on every branch."

On the afternoon of October 17 Ella Cooper arranged for her "Peaches" to have an interview with 'Abdu'l-Bahá. We were very happy and excited to think that we were to be in His presence and that He would speak to us. We went to His home and waited for Him to return from a walk. We were standing when He entered the room where we were to meet Him. I glanced at my friends, and seeing the expression of great anticipation on their radiant, smiling faces, I realized how joyfully we all had looked forward to this precious moment with the Master. He smiled as He welcomed us and seemed pleased to see a group of young ladies so eager to be with Him. I think that this was the first time that 'Abdu'l-Bahá had ever addressed a group composed only of young ladies. The Master gave a wonderful talk about "implements" which we should use for teaching the Faith:

> Be seated! How are you?
> We have been for a walk. San Francisco is a good city. San Francisco is a good garden, fresh and verdant. Skilled gardeners are needed to cultivate this garden, to plant fresh trees, to plant tender flowers, and to arrange delightful flower beds. The gardeners must then become birds, nightingales, and singing canaries, warbling melodiously in this garden.
> [To Ramona Allen] I have instructed you with your friends how to teach. You must act in accordance with my teachings, and then confirmations will attend your efforts. At each season a certain work is especially confirmed. The seasons differ, and at each specific season a special work is required and confirmed. There is a time for seed sowing. There is a time for irrigation. There is a time for the care of the harvest, and there is a time for the ultimate fruitage. In the time for seed sowing, whosoever sows seeds is confirmed, but if at that time, you should seek to reap, you would find no

harvest. There is a time for irrigation, and then that work is confirmed, but if you should wish to harrow, it is good, but it would be out of place. There is a time for reaping, when that work is confirmed, but if you should sow seeds or irrigate at that time, it would not be confirmed. There is a time for harvesting, and then that is confirmed.

Now is the time when no confirmations descend except for seed sowing. Whosoever sows seeds at this time is confirmed—that is, whosoever teaches is confirmed. That means that whosoever sows the seeds of faith in the fertile soil of hearts, such a one is confirmed.

The friends of GOD are all sowers. They are all gardeners. He who is the most accomplished sower, and who gardens most successfully, will reap the greatest results. If the gardener be not skilled, he will gather no harvest. If the sower be not skilled, although he labor very hard, he will reap no harvest. Therefore, each one of you must endeavor to become a skilled sower, a skilled gardener, so that many harvests may be gathered.

The gardeners of GOD need certain implements wherewith they may work well.

The first implement, the most essential one, is severance. Severance means that the heart must be detached from the things of the world. By this I do not mean that man must not have a business, that he must not be occupied, that he must not be in commerce. In this dispensation, these things constitute devotion. It is incumbent upon every man to be occupied; but his heart must be free and detached. Occupation is identical with devotion.

The second implement is the love of GOD. This is the great implement. It is the implement that ploughs the ground. The soil which was hidden beneath will be thrown out, and the surface soil will go down. In this manner the soil of the hearts is fertilized and blessed.

The third implement is the knowledge of GOD. When the servant becomes awakened to the knowledge of GOD and confirmed therein, then he can teach.

The fourth implement is endeavor. The servant must endeavor. Without endeavor he can accomplish nothing.

The fifth implement is praiseworthy attributes. The teacher must be adorned with infinite virtues, and his attributes must be radiant.

The sixth implement is eloquence. The servant must be possessed of eloquence.

When possessed of all these implements, he is a real gardener and he will gather many harvests. The trees will yield fruit and the meadows will become glorified.

When 'Abdu'l-Bahá had finished speaking my heart was filled with happiness and warm love for Him. We departed with the lingering memory of the Master's words, spoken in His soft, beautiful voice, so kindly uttering His instructions to us. Silently I prayed that the hearts of my dear friends had been touched by meeting 'Abdu'l-Bahá, and I hoped with all my heart that they had been inspired to follow His Teachings and be forever under His shadow.

Addressing the friends from Seattle and Portland on another occasion, 'Abdu'l-Bahá said:

> I am exceedingly happy to see you. Your faith is as the faith of Peter when His Holiness Christ addressed him thus: "Thou art Peter and upon this rock I will build my church."
>
> Praise be to God you are believers and assured. You are firm and confident. Faith must be like a rock. It must be like a mountain which withstands every torrent, test, and trial.
>
> I am very pleased with the believers in California and the states surrounding. I witness that they are believers in Reality. Their faith is cordial, not only faith by mere words. No differences exist among them. The utmost unity and accord prevail, and on this account I am exceedingly rejoiced, for the aim of the appearance of

the Manifestation of God has been to bring the dawn of the light of love. If there is no love among the believers of God, as it ought and should be, then how can they establish that love among the children of humanity?

His Holiness Christ, addressing His disciples said: "Ye are the salt of the earth: but if the salt hath lost its savor, wherewith shall it be salted?" Now if the believers of God do not exercise the utmost love and fellowship amongst each other, and if they are not united and harmonious, and if they are not attracted to each other, then how can they bring about that universal era of brotherhood and love?

I am exceedingly pleased with the believers of California and the other Western states. You must establish a bond of unity and agreement among yourselves to such extent that you may love each other.

If a believer enter a city, the believers of that city must receive him with the utmost cordiality. They must be happy that one of the believers of God has entered into that city. They must show him the greatest hospitality, present him in their assembly, and exercise toward him the utmost kindness and consideration. This is the qualification of the Bahá'ís. It is My utmost hope that you may be assisted therein.

In Persia such a state of love exists among the Bahá'ís that they are ready to sacrifice their lives for each other, and they have such an ideal communication like unto communication of flowers gathered together in a bouquet. This is the condition of the Bahá'ís, and this is befitting their claims and love.

I am exceedingly pleased with you all, and praise be to God you are exercising love and unity among yourselves.

It is customary, among the Persians, when they have visitors to offer something to eat.

'Abdu'l-Bahá then distributed a basket of fruit among the friends. Some of those present had questions they wished to ask of Him.

Mrs. Latimer: We have come to supplicate for those loved ones in Portland asking if He [the Master] could come north.

'Abdu'l-Bahá: I have the utmost longing to meet the friends there. For this purpose I have crossed the great length of the continent; and from Syria did I come to this state. My longing to meet them is inexpressible. But it is impossible: I must go.

I am very well pleased with you. Convey to the believers of God my Abhá greetings. I will pray for them. They are in my heart. With my spirit do I associate with them. Physical meeting has no importance. The meeting is spiritual. Therefore, they should not be unhappy. They should be rejoiced. . . .

For the Seattle Assembly: I ask special blessings, and I bring a greeting from Abhá.

The Assembly at Seattle is under the protection of the Blessed Perfection.

Mrs. Monroe: . . . what to do in the future to make me more worthy in the Cause?

'Abdu'l-Bahá: Walk in My pathway. Observe how day and night I am engaged in serving the Cause.

One evening the friends gathered in the drawing room of the Goodall home, and the Master told us of His visit to the beach in San Francisco. He said that all humanity is like the sea: at times it is smooth; at other times it is in motion. He said that the sea in motion is most like life, even when it is violent. When the sea is in motion, after a time, results occur. He said, " 'Seek to dive in the spiritual sea and bring up pearls; seek to find that sea.' "[19]

Another time 'Abdu'l-Bahá spoke of musical instruments, observing that all are imperfect instruments but that Bahá'u'lláh brought to earth a heavenly, divine instrument whereon each soul could find and strike his own note, and whose music would be a heavenly, eternal chorus.[20]

My mother had several interviews with the Master.

During one of them, at His home in San Francisco on the 21st of October, she asked about Bahá'í service.

> Mrs. Allen: I want to consecrate my life to the service of Bahá'u'lláh. Have I the capacity?
> 'Abdu'l-Bahá: Because you have this intention, that is capacity. The intention is capacity. If you did not have this intention, you would not ask for the capacity.
> Mrs. Allen: I want to know if my home in Berkeley may become a Bahá'í Center with your blessing?
> 'Abdu'l-Bahá: Very good. The very fact that you wish to have your home in Berkeley as a Bahá'í Center is an indication of capacity. May God aid you and bless you and that which is your intention may be achieved.

For many years after that my mother held Bahá'í meetings in our home.

That afternoon the Master spoke to Mr. Takeshi Kanno, who was a poet and well-known sculptor:

> The war between Japan and Russia came about after the departure of Bahá'u'lláh, but before these events occurred Bahá'u'lláh often mentioned kindly the name of the Mikado and his people, saying that among the reigning monarchs of the world he was distinguished. He was constantly thinking of the upbuilding of the country. He willingly passed over his own authority and despotic rules so that the country and the people might progress.

On another occasion, 'Abdu'l-Bahá spoke about devotion to the Cause:

> This is a meeting, the members of which are strung together like pearls, and all the pearls are brilliant, for all are Bahá'ís. The brilliancy of these pearls is not known for the present; that will be known later on.
> Thank ye God that He has drawn you together

through the Blessed Perfection. He has made you fruitful, like unto trees: He has made you like unto a rose garden, the freshness of which will be known in the future. When the heat and the rays of the Sun of Reality shine in the future, then the freshness and beauty of these flowers will be realized.

In brief, render thanks to God, for your spirits are gladdened with the glad tidings of God. Be forgetful of all other thoughts. Be filled with the Spirit of Bahá'u'lláh. Your thoughts must be of Bahá'u'lláh; your mention must be of Bahá'u'lláh; your life must be devoted to Bahá'u'lláh; your firmness must be evident in Bahá'u'lláh; for Bahá'u'lláh has endured for your sake infinite vicissitudes. All His life He was subject to persecutions. During the nights He was not at rest. He did not sleep in peace for one night—not one. Never did He find peace and composure. All His life He was subject to persecution. All His life He was exiled. All His life He was imprisoned.

Therefore, we must be loyal to Him, turn our faces to Him, praise His mention in this world, expound His Teachings, quicken people with His Spirit, so that His Heavenly Image may descend and His Heavenly Power affect the hearts. Thus, every day may we find a new spirit. Every day may we make a new resolution. Every day may we be confirmed, and illumine the world of humanity.

We must supplicate day and night, beg assistance and confirmation from His Holiness Bahá'u'lláh, that we may become pure mirrors, that the rays of sincerity may perfect them, the virtues of the human world appear, the moralities of the Kingdom be reflected, and that we may attain the high station of happiness.

This is My advice to you. This is My request for you. This is My hope for you.

One day I spoke to a young man about 'Abdu'l-Bahá and the Teachings of Bahá'u'lláh, telling him that due to the power of the clergy and rulers of Persia and Turkey He had been, with His Father and Family, imprisoned for over forty years.[21] Despite this, when 'Abdu'l-Bahá was released from prison, He traveled to spread His Father's Faith from 'Akká to San Francisco. As we parted that evening, my friend said to me, "Ramona, I believe in these Teachings, and I accept 'Abdu'l-Bahá as the leader of this Faith." I was astonished that my friend had so quickly accepted the Teachings. He was Joseph Grandin Bray, one day to become my husband and the father of my two children, Allen and Barbara.

On one very happy occasion Ella arranged for 'Abdu'l-Bahá to speak to the "Peaches" and their young men friends in His home. I invited Joseph Bray. The Master spoke to us of the very important role which Bahá'í youth would be called upon to play in that day and in the future. Then the Master spoke about two kinds of teaching:

> About teaching. You may teach in two ways. One way is limited teaching; another way is the unlimited teaching.
>
> Teaching in a limited way consists of the following, namely: explaining the proofs and evidences in regard to the principles of Bahá'u'lláh, quoting prophecies from the Old and New Testaments, stating that that Day has come. Moreover the intellectual proofs and evidences are this and this, etc. The principles of Bahá'u'lláh have been set forth with such potency and penetration that no one can deny them. While He was in prison, He was in chains, and He wrote important Epistles to the Kings and Rulers of the world. All that which He wrote in these letters came to pass later on. The Tablets of Bahá'u'lláh do exist quoting therein wonderful signs which appeared to Bahá'u'lláh during the various periods of His life.
>
> While in prison He withstood two despotic kings, and He gained victory over both. In prison He raised His Banner, He spread His Teachings and spiritually defeated two despotic kings. They could not prevent the spread of His Teachings. In brief, while in prison, He raised the Ensign of His Principles. This is impaneled in the history of the world. Such dominion appeared from

Him, and such potency manifested from His personality. There are many instances of such, and when a person explains these things, He is guiding, He is teaching, He is crying out. This is teaching in a limited sense.

Teaching in an unlimited sense consists of the following and is very good, very great: the teacher himself (or herself) becomes the standing proof of Bahá'u'lláh—that he (or she) may become a miracle of Bahá'u'lláh with such power and such knowledge and desire, such actions and such words and character, and such heavenly powers, that you may live amongst the people, that you may be a proof, undeniable proof, of Bahá'u'lláh.

If someone ask: "What is the proof of Bahá'u'lláh?" one may say such a person—there is the proof; look at her. Bahá'u'lláh has educated this person. He has awakened this soul. He has quickened this life. He has made this person a speaker; He has given her knowledge, made her holy, made her sanctified—a shining light—He has made her a sun.

This is the unlimited teaching.

God willing, each one of you may become a sun.

At that time in the Bay Area a very few young people besides the "Peach Tree" and two or three young men were interested in the Teachings. We were the youth of that day. How very thrilling it is to me to see many youth coming into the Faith and taking responsibility for teaching other youth. They are fortunate to have for study and teaching the advantage of the sacred Writings of Bahá'u'lláh and 'Abdu'l-Bahá (which have been translated by Shoghi Effendi), and of the many books written by the Guardian, by some of the Hands of the Cause, and by a few of the early believers. It gives me great happiness that two of my grandsons [David Lee and Richard Allen West] are busily engaged in Bahá'í activities.

One evening Joseph asked if we might have an interview with 'Abdu'l-Bahá. It was arranged by [Ella, our] "Mother Peach." The Master welcomed us warmly and invited us into a small room where, except for His interpreter, we were alone with Him. We stood before 'Abdu'l-Bahá while He spoke of the teaching work to be done in California—work that required firmness and steadfastness. He said we should pray ardently and each day spread the Message of Bahá'u'lláh. Then, looking kindly and lovingly at us, He asked us to tell Him what was in our hearts.

Words did not come easily, for we both felt the sacredness of that moment. 'Abdu'l-Bahá walked a few steps from us, then came back, and again said, "Tell Me what is in your hearts." He looked at us in such a tender manner that my heart was deeply touched. He then listened intently while each of us expressed our thoughts and wishes. Afterwards, He spoke kindly and wisely of matters concerning us alone. Taking one of each of our hands in His and holding them gently, He said He would pray that we would both reach the apex of happiness.

After receiving a cable from 'Abdu'l-Bahá with His blessings, Joseph Bray and I were married in November 1916. "Mother Peach" was my matron of honor, and Joseph's brother, Arthur, was his best man. We were very happy in our Berkeley home where we held Bahá'í Feasts and meetings and where many outstanding Bahá'í teachers spoke of the Faith.

I am sure that Joe reached the apex of happiness in meeting 'Abdu'l-Bahá and through years of devoted, steadfast, self-sacrificing service to the Cause of Bahá'u'lláh until his untimely death in San Francisco on May 23, 1938.

The apex of my happiness has been reached over a period of many years in many ways. I have had the blessed privilege of being in the presence of the Master, of making a pilgrimage to Haifa as the guest of Shoghi Effendi, of having four generations of Bahá'ís in my family, and, above all, of being able to serve the Faith. The love, the guidance, and the blessings which the Master bestowed upon me and my family have been a guiding light throughout my life and will, I pray, continue into all the worlds of God.

In San Francisco my father, Dr. Woodson Allen, my brother, Dr. Warren Allen, and his best friend, Dr. Joseph Catton, had an interview with the Master at His home on the evening of October 21st. As all three were medical doctors, 'Abdu'l-Bahá spoke to them of healing:

'Abdu'l-Bahá: Did you have any questions, Dr. Allen?

Dr. Woodson Allen: I want to ask one question. Most of my life has been given to the study and practice of medicine and surgery, and ever in that field of activity I must look for the handiwork of God, and the question that is puzzling me is simply this: can I give a man any assurance that he can be healed through the power of the Holy Spirit? For instance, I tell a man that he needs a surgical operation and he immediately believes me, but if I say that I believe he might be healed through the power of the Holy Spirit he would probably say to me that I was a fanatic and go to some other doctor.

'Abdu'l-Bahá: Diseases are of two kinds. There are some which are due to material cause, and such diseases should be treated according to material methods. For instance, supposing there shall be some sort of process in the liver that is tissue pathology. Its treatment should be entirely physical. On the other hand, another disease may be *spiritual* in character. For example, fear is a nervous disease resulting not from any material cause. It is psychological neurosis. That sort of disease has to be treated spiritually.

God has not created all the plants you know and all the various metals for nothing. They are for some purpose. They have their physiologic findings, and each one of them has its physiologic result. They are not for useless purposes. And if we deny pharmaceutics and therapeutics, then it would mean that all these things are without physiologic effect, when there is use for each one of these plants. For example, if a man is stricken with fever, we will say with ague, if we give him quinine, it acts as a specific, and we know it is a remedy. Or a man may have smallpox, and we vaccinate him. We know vaccination is a preventive. Nobody can deny that. . . . You see that would be foolishness. Everything has its use and its place. A man may be stricken with a certain form of skin disease—psoriasis, for example, and we use a certain form of remedy. You cannot deny that sort of thing.

Can you deny the effect of these medicines? No! What do you think of that? Don't you think that is so?

Dr. Allen: It is true.

'Abdu'l-Bahá: But, on the other hand, there may be some diseases due to some spiritual cause. For example, a man may be subjected to excessive joy. Out of that excessive joy may result mental derangement—a sort of emotional shock. It will be an emotional upsetting. That has to be treated spiritually. Or, fear may cause a tremendous shock to the nervous system and then that should be treated according to psychotherapy. And so on. There are many diseases which are neuroses and have to be treated accordingly.

Suppose a man has an abscess that is suppurating. Unless we do something for that abscess, it may go and become gangrened; it may become diseased. Suppose we leave this abscess. If we say prayers over that abscess—the prayer for that is the knife—the surgeon's knife—it is the lance. We should lance it out.

You see both have their places. Those diseases that are due to psychological neurosis, treat them according to psychological neurosis and suggestive therapeutics, and those that are due to material causes then you have to give them the material treatment. For example, an abscess has to be incised. If you do not lance it, it will go on and become gangrenous, because the origin of that is entirely material pathology.

This is the truth of the matter: to discard medicine is nonsense. Medicine is perfectly reasonable.

Even the animals when they are sick, though they

are not intelligent, know where certain grasses grow, and nature leads them to certain herbs, and they taste those herbs, and they smell them, and certain grasses that seem to please their taste they eat and get well. This is natural is it not?

For example, when your finger is wounded, you naturally stick it in your mouth. Evidently the saliva has something to do with that and seems to act as a salve. The animals, whenever they have a wound, lick it with their tongue and get well. This is natural. This is not a process of thought.

There are a number of diseases which are psychological. They have to be treated according to suggestive therapeutics.

Your hand may become wounded. Suppose you just imagine that there is not a wound there. You say: "My hand is not wounded." Would that help it? Would that help it? Would that cure it? You agree with that, don't you?

Dr. Allen: There is one point I want to make. Take, for instance, a child that is sick. Everything has been done for the illness—in a surgical case—in a therapeutic way. The doctors have given up, but when some prayers are said for the child, it gets well. How is that?

The child had whooping cough. It got wet in the evening, and took cold and got pneumonia, and the doctor treated the child for several hours, and gave all the remedies he could think of, and the child kept getting worse. He called for me, and from all appearances it did not seem the child could possibly live. Every paroxysm seemed to be its last, and the pulse could not be felt at the wrist, and when it did come it was simply a flutter. He asked me what I thought, and I said I thought the child was dying. He said, what should we do? I suggested some simple remedy, and he gave that along with the one he had been giving. I sat by the child and took its hand, and said the Greatest Name, and in a few hours the child began to improve. As far as my mentality goes I cannot see that the remedy did the child any good.

The question that came to me is: Did the saying of the Greatest Name make it well?

In the morning, the doctor was tired, and he asked me if I would stay with the child while he went home. I stayed a few hours, and the child improved so well I went home, and the doctor called next morning and said: "That was wonderful medicine you gave the child, for the child is practically well."

Now, what I want to know is what cured that child?

Dr. Faríd: The Greatest Name.

Dr. Allen: That is what I want to know—how can I say that to those people?

'Abdu'l-Bahá: The first thing for us to find out is whether the two forms of treatment—the spiritual and material—are real or not. We must investigate that first: whether the material medicine, or spiritual medicine, has a basis for that or not; whether they are real or not. That is the foundation.

We find that in the creation of God there is a basis for material medicine. Even in the animals, which are devoid of thought, there is an instinct which propels them when they are sick. They go to certain herbs which are physiologically suited, and they eat them. That is one thing.

Secondly, a man may have malaria, and as soon as we give him quinine it seems to have its specific effect; or, in diarrhea, opium has its effect, stopping it; or, in psoriasis, if we give a form of mercurial treatment, it may heal it; or, in the case of a wound, if we wash it with carbolic acid, it gets well. So you see there is a basis for material medicine. We cannot deny that. It is not so?

Then we come to the spiritual medicine. We find that it often happens that a man gets sick, and we pray, and he gets well. It often happens. That happens in numerous cases. A man has become insane, and we pray, and he gets well. It often has happened. A man has, day by day, become emaciat-

'ABDU'L-BAHÁ
with friends from many cities,
including some of the "Peach Tree,"
gathered for the Feast on October 16, 1912,
at the home of Helen Goodall in Oakland, California.

Views of the balcony and stained glass window in the home of Helen Goodall in Oakland, California, where 'Abdu'l-Bahá stood and chanted a benediction after the Feast on October 16, 1912.

'ABDU'L-BAHÁ
walking in front of the home of Helen Goodall
in Oakland, California, on October 23, 1912.

*photograph
courtesy
Ramona Brown*

'ABDU'L-BAHÁ
in front of the Goodall home on October 23, 1912,
talking with friends, including a group of East Indian students
who had attended Frances Orr Allen's Bahá'í classes in Berkeley.

*photograph
courtesy
Ramona Brown*

ed, and we pray, and he gets well, gets strength. And so on in many cases.

Therefore, both of these have their provinces. Hence, both of them should be used—both the one material and the other the spiritual. Neither of them has to be given up.

Dr. Catton: The doctor wanted to know whether this whooping cough, which is a material thing, was benefitted by a spiritual thing. (To Dr. Fareed) Does he want to treat the material side with material things?

'Abdu'l-Bahá: It is possible to treat not *every* material, not *all* the material. Some can be treated spiritually. There can be some spiritual disease and material medicine will help it. Both are possible. The spiritual can help the material, too. But there are some diseases that are material that must receive entirely material or physical treatment, just like an abscess, for example. While an abscess is coming to a head, is suppurating—that has to be lanced. But before inflammation has set in, and it is not suppurating, the beginning of it can properly be treated spiritually, but when suppuration has taken place, then you have to lance; otherwise it will become gangrenous, because it is already corrupted—it has to be evacuated. For example, suppose there is an abscess in My hand, suppuration has taken place, and the hand is swollen and has come to a heading. It has to be evacuated.

Dr. Catton: Then the spiritual side can protect the side which is not destroyed? You can hope to cure *diseased* tissue, but not destroyed tissue?

'Abdu'l-Bahá: Sometimes a disease may become very predominant, like melancholia. That can be spiritually cured. Most of the nervous diseases can be treated spiritually, because they are psychical.

Dr. Catton: The question is the spiritual curing of the material. I want to draw the line where you can cure and where you cannot. Take a given cell in the body, and start to treat it wrongly, so as to destroy it. Up to a certain place, that cell can still be brought back to life: past a certain stage, it dies. Where it is capable of regeneration, can it be cured spiritually?

Dr. Faríd: There is no line of demarcation.

Dr. Catton: An abscess is only a stage in the disease of a material thing, and if there is a general underlying law that spiritual treatment should be employed to treat material things, it does not seem right that there should be a stage where spiritual treatment is of no use, unless you come to a stage where the tissue is actually destroyed.

'Abdu'l-Bahá: Is there any law which is not limited? God alone is unlimited. There is no process which is not limited. For instance, whether spiritual or material, can you hinder a man from dying? Therefore, it is limited.

Dr. Catton: Spiritual treatment will help a man that is alive and will not help a man who is dying?

'Abdu'l-Bahá: Use both of them. Do not limit. Use both, and get results.

(To Dr. Allen) I gave you spiritual treatment. I will tell you that. When you came to me, you were sick. You are quite well now. Without letting you know I treated you. Your pulse was not so good. Your pulse is improved, and now you are a different man. Get up and look in the looking glass. I did not let you know about it.

The spiritual treatment has its effect, of course. I am not saying that this is impossible to be treated spiritually. I am saying that all these are to be used. Pray and give medicine, too. You pray that the medicine will work, and the medicine will work. One of them will do it.

It is very humorous!

The people who say medicine is not right . . . are off. If a man gets hungry, he has to have food. He cannot say: "I am not hungry." If he says: "I am not hungry," he does not get satisfied, because hunger is a sort of disease, too. Or, if he says: "I am not thirsty," will his thirst be quenched, do you think? Likewise sleep. If he is sleepy and says: "I am not sleepy," and affirms he is not sleepy, he still wants sleep. That is natural.

The point is this, that when a man is hungry, or thirsty, give him his bread and water, his food. There is a void that has to be filled, and something has to go there. A vacuum is there. Give him water. Praying over it will not fill him.

Good-bye. Bless you! Bless you!

In 1912, when He told us this, doctors generally did not use or perhaps understand the method of healing through psychological means. Dr. Warren Allen became an outstanding neurosurgeon, and Dr. Joseph Catton became a well-known psychiatrist in the Bay Area.

'Abdu'l-Bahá invited my father and me to visit Him one evening at His home in San Francisco. When we entered His room, the Master was reclining against the pillows on His bed, and one of His secretaries was massaging His feet and ankles. The Master explained that His feet caused Him great pain, which was eased by massage. We knew that 'Abdu'l-Bahá suffered much as a result of frostbite from walking and riding in the snow during the exile of the Holy Family in Turkey, and also because of the heavy chains which He had been forced to wear part of the time on His ankles while in prison.

The Master greeted us most cordially and lovingly, smiled His wonderful smile, and invited my father to be seated. I stood with my arm over my father's shoulder. They spoke of conditions in the world and of many other things. 'Abdu'l-Bahá, knowing that my father was a physician and surgeon, suddenly said:

Dr. Allen, *you* understand healing. You *understand* healing. You understand *healing*! You know that many diseases can be cured through simple medicines and remedies and by suggestions to the patients, but when there is an abscess on the hand you must cut it out and clean it so that it will heal. [He demonstrated with His hands.] You understand there is spiritual healing and material healing, and unless these two work together, a cure is impossible. The material healing is surgery and medicine, and the spiritual healing is of God.

'Abdu'l-Bahá continued to explain the methods of healing which would be used in the future, such as the use of varying temperatures of water and the eating of fruits, vegetables, and nuts.

My father often suffered severe attacks of asthma. When their conversation was finished I asked 'Abdu'l-Bahá what I could do to help my father when he was ill. The Master looked at me and smiled in an amused way. Then He became very serious and said: "Rub him. Rub him." Many times after that interview I relieved my father's suffering by rubbing him. At the moment of his death in 1918 I was rubbing his forehead. In a vision at the moment my father died, I saw 'Abdu'l-Bahá come toward my father with a wonderful smile and with arms extended, and embrace him, welcoming him into the Abhá Kingdom. As they walked away the Master put His arm around my father's shoulder; then they turned, smiled, and my father said: "Tell Warren to have no regrets that he is not here. Tell him to call upon me in moments of need, and I will help him always." 'Abdu'l-Bahá led my father to His chair, a handsome, high-backed, throne-like chair of a light brown material, elaborately carved, and with dark green velvet on the back and arms. He seated my father in His chair and stood near him. Both were smiling lovingly. Then my vision vanished.

Shortly before this Warren had left for Europe to serve as a neurosurgeon in World War I. He told us later that he was in France, walking down a street with a friend, when he turned to his friend and asked, "What time is it?" The friend answered. Then Warren said, "My father has just died." When Warren returned to his quarters that evening, he found a cable stating that our father had died at exactly that hour.

Warren told me that several times in his practice he remembered the promise our father had made and called upon him for assistance, always receiving the help and guidance he sought. Recalling one such incident, Warren told me that one day he had been called to the hospital to see a boy about nine years old who had what was diagnosed to be a dangerous brain tumor. The parents had been to a prominent neurosurgeon in San Francisco who told them that he could do nothing for their boy and suggested that they consult Dr. Allen. As Warren stood at the child's bedside, he realized that it would be practically impossible to operate on him with the hospital's existing facilities. He knew that he must help him, but how?

Warren went and sat in his car and tried to think of some way in which he could possibly operate. Suddenly he recalled Father's promise that in time of need, if Warren prayed and called on him for help, he would answer. Then, as a picture before him, Warren saw a most unusual operating table. It was the answer to his dilemma! The hospital built the table according to his instructions, and Warren was able to perform on the boy what was said to be a miraculous operation. The boy lived and after many, many months of patient therapy was able to take his place with children of his own age.

Another time, after the war in Europe was over and Warren had returned home, a very prominent man living in Texas who had been a close friend and former patient of my father's, became very ill with a throat infection. He required a very serious operation and insisted upon traveling to Oakland to be under Warren's care. Everything went well during the operation until suddenly a problem arose. Warren hesitated a second, perhaps with a tinge of apprehension and the realization of his responsibility for the success of the operation. Then he remembered the promise Father had made. He prayed, and then he felt assured that all would be well. Warren completed the brilliant operation, after which the patient recovered fully. These two accounts from my brother serve as further proof to me that, when we make ourselves open channels through prayer and meditation, God can work through us, and our departed loved ones can aid us.

On October 22 'Abdu'l-Bahá spoke to an audience of children gathered at His home on California Street.[22] Passing from one to another, the Master gave each child two handsful of marshmallows, saying, "Two hands, two hands." Then He addressed the children:

> May God assist and comfort all of them. Good children, good children. I am pleased with meeting the children. They are the plants of the Rose Garden of Abhá. I will pray to God that He may bestow upon them a Bahá'í training and education so that each one of them may become a very good Bahá'í. They are very good children, excellent children. They are all illumined.

On the morning of October 23, at the home of Helen Goodall, I asked if I might take two of my best friends to meet 'Abdu'l-Bahá. They were Marie Barr and Betty Vent, both members of the "Peach Tree" group. Marie and I had been friends since we were four years old, and years later we married brothers. We still enjoy our friendship.

When we entered the room, 'Abdu'l-Bahá was seated in a large comfortable chair, and we three sat in a large chair opposite Him. He welcomed us with His beautiful smile and began speaking to us about teaching the Faith. Marie told Him that she did not have a college education and, therefore, did not feel qualified to teach the Faith. He told her not to be concerned, saying: "When you wish to teach, turn your heart to Bahá'u'lláh, and say what enters your mind."

'Abdu'l-Bahá seemed pleased that we were serious and anxious to have Him instruct us. He answered our questions graciously and courteously, always with a loving smile and warm understanding of the enthusiasm of youth. Sometimes He nodded His head as His words were being translated. He was happy to see these youth show their love for Him, their eagerness to serve Him and to learn from Him by absorbing His every word and gesture. The Master often laughed when He was speaking to the "Peach Tree" and on other occasions as well. I knew He was not laughing at us but with us. He had a fine sense of humor. Once 'Abdu'l-Bahá laughed so heartily at our questions and observations that His turban became disarranged. As He lifted His hands to straighten it, He smiled as though we had a little joke between us. Then the Master said:

>   Welcome, very welcome.
>   These young ladies have asked Me how to teach and the method of teaching. I have told them a few days ago, and now I will recapitulate.
>   You must first be assured of the fact that whosoever heralds the Cause of God, the Kingdom of Abhá, will be confirmed. This has been tried heretofore. Whosoever has stepped forth in this arena, the hosts of the Supreme Concourse have aided. He has been confirmed and assisted. He has achieved extraordinary progress. Upon him the door of Knowledge has been opened. His eyes were opened, and the Breath of the Holy Spirit aided him, and he was instrumental in guiding others. It has been tried. No one has advanced toward this Cause without receiving this confirmation.
>   Secondly: when a man sings a beautiful melody, he, himself, more than his audience, will be moved by his song. Hence, when a man commences guiding souls, when he expounds the Teachings, he, himself, will experience keenly the sense of joy.
>   Thirdly: everything in the world of existence is limited. There is nothing which is unlimited, except the eternal confirmation of God, and that eternal confirmation of God through teaching, will be attained by man.
>   Consequently, His Holiness Christ says, when you speak that which is in your heart, you are inspired to say, that you must expound, and that is the Breath of the Holy Spirit. Therefore, I say to you, and to all of you: If you seek the eternal Bestowal, teach. If you seek entrance at the Threshold of God, teach. If you seek eternal glory, teach. If you wish to win eternal life, teach. If you wish the supremacy of heaven, teach. And be confident that confirmation will attend you and that Divine assistance will uphold you. Because it has been tried many, many times.

But it requires firmness, it requires steadfastness. Consider the disciples of Christ, and their steadfastness. They were exposed to the sword, and they were not afraid; they were firm and steadfast. When a man drinks from a fount of salubrious waters, naturally he wants to convey the water to others. If a man reaches a tree bearing luscious fruits, he wishes to enjoy them with others. If a man hears a beautiful voice, he wishes others to hear it also.

If you seek to attain the everlasting bounties, and occupy yourselves conveying the message of God, and to be the means of guiding souls, do not look at your capacity, do not look at your dessert. If Peter had looked at his own capacity, he would have remained a fisherman. He was quite devoid of knowledge. But he did not look at his own capacity. Nay, rather, he looked at the divine bounty. And you must not look at your own capacity. You must not say that you are young, that you have not entered college, that you have not attained an extraordinary education. Nay, rather, consider the bounties of the Kingdom of Abhá. What beautiful fruits are produced by the black soil. This is not due to the capacity of the soil, but because of the great heat of the sun and of the rain from the clouds. Likewise, you must not say that you are dust. Nay, rather, you must look at the effulgence of the Sun of Reality, which ever shines upon you. You must look at the cloud of the Kingdom that ever pours down its rain upon you. You must feel the breeze of Providence that ever blows toward you.

We three sat spellbound as 'Abdu'l-Bahá impressed upon us in simple and beautiful language the great importance of teaching the Faith and assured us of wonderful confirmations. For a moment, as we remained seated, I silently prayed that I would ever remain firm and steadfast. Then we stood, and just as the Master started to leave the room, I asked Him what I should teach. He smilingly replied, "Memorize the talk I gave at Stanford University." His answer left me breathless; I had heard

Him give that lecture on October 8 and now realized what an important talk it was to use in teaching. Many times later the Master was asked how to teach, and He would reply: "Teach as I teach. Teach as I teach!" To me this means teaching not only with words but with the deeds of our daily lives.

After the interview with 'Abdu'l-Bahá was over, we followed Him downstairs and out to the sidewalk, as He wished to walk in the California sunshine He so enjoyed. Soon the Master was surrounded by a group of friends, among them some East Indian students who were studying at the University of California. I approached 'Abdu'l-Bahá and asked permission to take His photograph, which He granted. When my picture was printed, it showed a group of people standing with the Master, but only He was surrounded by a light which covered His head and shoulders. In both Europe and America whenever I have this photograph printed the photographers invariably ask what kind of flash I used to take the picture. I reply that I took the photograph in 1912 before the time of flash bulbs and I had used only a simple Brownie box camera. Moreover, I took the picture on a morning when the sun was shining upon all alike. When the *Tablets of Abdul-Baha* were published I found a reference He made to a picture of Himself possibly bearing some relation to my extraordinary photograph of Him:

> "Verily, thou hast seen the physical picture of Abdul-Baha printed by the rays of the phenomenal sun (*i.e.*, his photograph) and thine eyes became overflowing with tears. Beg thou of God that He may show unto thee his (Abdul-Baha's) spiritual picture printed by the ray shining forth from the Merciful Kingdom. Then the attractions of God shall overtake thee and make thee as a spark of fire aflame with the heat of the love of God."[23]

After a few minutes the Master walked away from the Group, and I caught a picture of Him strolling alone in front of Mrs. Goodall's home.

On the morning of October 24 the friends from Seattle gathered in the house of the Master. He greeted them, saying:

All are welcome; all are very welcome!

I was longing to see you very much. Praise be to God you came, and here we are meeting. For us to meet is one of the greatest favors of God, as the fire of yearning flames in every heart; and I offer thanks to the Kingdom of Abhá that this was made feasible. He brought many of you from a distant country here. He aided you to come and be present, and made it possible for us to assemble and be here, seated in the utmost of love and to speak thus. Thereby, the means of happiness is afforded, and it should make all of you very happy.

The Glad Tidings of the Kingdom of Abhá are abroad, the summons of Bahá'u'lláh is aloft, the Sun of Reality is shining, the cloud of mercy is showering, the breezes of Providence are blowing, and the graces of God from every standpoint are revealed.

Therefore, we should be very joyous indeed, very grateful. We must ever thank God.

How many people were the souls that dwelt in the city of Bahá'u'lláh, how many souls that were traveling on the journey with Bahá'u'lláh, and just as Christ says: "A prophet is not without honor save in his own country," they were deprived, and you who are from this distant region have attained. You have become intimate with the mysteries. Consider what a bestowal He has revealed, what a bounty He has conferred upon you.

From various regions of the world, hosts and hosts are entering the Kingdom of God. I pray for you daily, seeking for yours ideal progress, requesting for you the power of insight, the enlargement of your perceptions, that ideal bounties may continuously reach you and that all of you shall advance along all the degrees of endeavor, towards God's perfection.

May you become illumined, each as candles through the Light of Guidance, and like unto an ocean—by the winds of the love of God shall you surge. May you become green and fresh and verdant by the breezes of the favor of God. May you yield the fruits of the Kingdom, being the cause of guidance to the people of the earth. Such is my hope.

Praise be to God, you have heard the summons of the Kingdom; you have witnessed the bounty of the outpouring of Abhá; you have advanced to the Kingdom; and you have acquired a power from the Great Guidance. You have become radiant. . . .

Be happy. Do not weep. Be happy. You should be joyous. I hope that day by day you will advance in ideal ways, that you may progress every instant. Thus may you attain to that which is the superlative desire of the saints and holy ones.

This is My greatest wish for you.

Speaking further to one of the Seattle friends, Mr. King, 'Abdu'l-Bahá said:

Unless a man give his whole thought to a subject, he cannot comprehend it fully. He must give his mind to the thing, be free, and then he will understand it. You will know it fully. When a pupil enters the school first, he will not understand a thing at all, but when he persists in his studies, he will learn his first lessons. Even so it is with the Kingdom of God. When a person enters, when he concentrates his thought and is steadfast, he will learn good lessons, very good lessons indeed.

Tuesday evening, October 24, the friends all gathered at the home of Helen Goodall.[24] It was to be our farewell meeting with 'Abdu'l-Bahá, and our hearts were heavy at the thought of the separation. When we entered the room, the Master was seated. There was a reverent silence as He started speaking in soft tones. Again, He seemed enveloped in a golden light, and His face reflected love and sweetness. He repeated how happy He was to be with the friends in California and that our love had drawn Him to us. He praised the friends for spreading and establishing the Faith. He said He had done what He could to spread His Father's Revelation. He offered us good cheer and hope, and assured us of His prayers at the Holy Shrines.

One felt His great humility as He told of Bahá'u'lláh's life and suffering, His banishment with His Family from Írán, their native land. Tears filled His eyes and ran down His cheeks, and with a catch in His voice He told of the deprivations and hardships endured by His beloved Father and Family and the little band of followers who had accompanied them. He said that during their exile from Constantinople to Adrianople, they had to walk in the snow. His delicate Mother, Navváb, was forced to melt ice to get water for drinking and for washing clothes. He reminded us of the two years of lonely solitude Bahá'u'lláh had spent in Sulaymáníyyih, and He said that Bahá'u'lláh's only aim was to unite mankind. The Master seemed to be reliving those days of heartbreak. Sadness filled our hearts; tears streamed down our faces while He told us of the cruelties and great injustices inflicted upon His Father. In that quiet room one felt the love and deep sympathy pouring from our souls to our blessed 'Abdu'l-Bahá.

All at once His voice became strong and firm, His eyes luminous, and with great authority He told of the Declaration of Bahá'u'lláh in the Garden of Riḍván—that He was the Promised One for this day! He told how later, in 'Akká, Bahá'u'lláh gave the Principles of His Revelation and explained that the establishment of His Covenant would forever safeguard His Cause. 'Abdu'l-Bahá said that His Father had written: "'. . . I have appointed one who is the Center of my Covenant. All must obey him; all must turn to him; he is the expounder of my book. . . .'"[25]

Suddenly the atmosphere in the room became electrified. 'Abdu'l-Bahá rose majestically from His chair and in a powerful voice declared: "I am the Center of that Covenant! I am the Center of that Covenant!" The friends stood up. They seemed stunned by this great announcement and filled with indescribable emotion. Wonder, joy, and happiness showed in their faces. Gradually we became aware in Whose presence we stood: "The Mystery of God," God's special gift to all mankind. Several moments passed before 'Abdu'l-Bahá spoke again. Then, looking at each one, almost pleading, He asked those who believed to spread the Teachings, to be firm and steadfast, to teach not by words alone but by deeds. He said, "These wonderful days are passing swiftly; and, once gone, they will never come again."

When He finished speaking, we knew that our last meeting with our beloved Master was over. The moment of parting had come. As we passed before Him, one by one, with tears in our eyes, and filled with emotion, He took each of us by the hand, smiled into our eyes, and uttered the Greatest Name in farewell.

On the morning of October 25 the friends gathered to bid 'Abdu'l-Bahá good-bye at the Mole, the railroad terminal in Oakland from which His train would depart. He was to stop in Sacramento to meet the friends there and speak at two public meetings before proceeding to New York. Despite the pleas of the believers the Master was seated in a chair car. As usual He refused the comfort of a Pullman, saying, "We are the army of God." The friends crowded near Him; each one seemed to long for a few last words with 'Abdu'l-Bahá. My cousin, Cathryn, and I were standing near Him, happy just to be in His presence a few minutes longer.

Suddenly we looked at each other with the same thought. I said, "Let's go to Sacramento!" We discussed it only a moment, for at once we realized that the train was moving. The decision had been made for us; we were on our way to Sacramento. Imagine how excited and happy we were to be traveling in the same car as the Master! Ella Cooper and a few other believers were accompanying Him for the last hours of His visit in California.

When 'Abdu'l-Bahá and His party arrived in Sacramento, to His astonishment He was driven to the home of one of the Bahá'ís, where Ella had arranged a luncheon for a group of ladies. During luncheon the Master conversed with the ladies; He listened to their questions, answered them, told a few amusing stories, then excused Himself and retired to a room to rest. Then He sent for Ella. She told me: "He was reclining on the bed when I entered. He said to me: 'What have you done? The friends are waiting for me at the hotel!' I knelt by His bedside and wept bitterly, for He scolded me so hard I thought my heart would break. Then the Master said: 'Never again arrange anything for 'Abdu'l-Bahá without first consulting Him. Now we must go. You have kept the friends waiting for Me too long.'" Later, the Master comforted Ella with the compassion which He showed for everyone in sorrow or trouble. He gave comfort to all, and everyone felt the warmth of His deep love. He said constantly: "No tears! No tears! Be happy! Be happy!"

In the Master's first public address in Sacramento, He spoke of the followers of His Holiness Christ and how they were with Jesus, watching and observing His conduct and thoughts. They saw the persecutions which were heaped upon Him. Then, after His ascension, they scattered the teachings and instructions which Jesus had given them. "Through their instrumentality the east was illumined and the light . . . flooded the west. . . . Through His Holiness Christ the oneness of the world of humanity received its expression and proved to be the cause of spiritual illumination for mankind. The breaths of the Holy Spirit became effective in the hearts of people."[26]

'Abdu'l-Bahá explained that He had come from the Orient to announce the appearance of Bahá'u'lláh:

> We have observed his life and beheld his deeds. We have been witnesses of his ordeals and sufferings; observers of his imprisonment and exile. . . . Therefore we who are his disciples have been scattered throughout the world in order that his teachings may be widespread and be heard by every ear. Thus may the people receive the glad-tidings of the dawn of his great dispensation, become aware of the divine evidences manifest in him, be informed . . . of the might of his spirit in upholding under all circumstances the standard of the oneness of the world of mankind.[27]

The Master gave a brief epitome of Bahá'u'lláh's life in order that all would be informed of the history of His great Revelation and know His Teachings.

'Abdu'l-Bahá had luncheon with some of the friends in Sacramento. He spoke to them of His love for them and His hope that they would spread the Faith, sowing seeds—as He did—everywhere He went. He said, "The greatest bestowal of God to man is the capacity to attain human virtues."

Early on the morning of October 26 Mrs. Latimer told the Master of a message which she had brought for Him from some Japanese believers in Portland, Oregon. Replying to them through her, 'Abdu'l-Bahá said: "Convey on My behalf kindness to each one of them, and say that Mrs. Latimer conveyed to Me your message. I am exceedingly pleased with you and have prayed for you that God will surround you with His Heavenly confirmation and assistance. Rest assured that He will surround you with His bounties."

On that same day the Master spoke to a large audience at the Hotel Sacramento, saying in part:

> may the people of California become the most exalted and perfect altruists of the world. California is indeed a blessed country. . . . The Californians are a noble people; therefore I hope they may make extraordinary progress and become renowned for their virtues. . . .
>
> Inasmuch as the Californians seem peace-loving and possessed of great worthiness and capacity, I hope that advocates of peace may daily increase among them until the whole population shall stand for that beneficent outcome. May the men of affairs in this democracy uphold the standard of international conciliation. Then may altruistic aims and thoughts radiate from this center toward all other regions of the earth and may the glory of this accomplishment forever halo the history of this country. May the first flag of International Peace be upraised in this State. May the first illumination of reality shine gloriously upon this soil. May this center

and capitol become distinguished. . . . for the virtues of humanity and the possibilities of human advancement are boundless.[28]

I heard 'Abdu'l-Bahá utter these words in Sacramento in 1912. Imagine my great happiness when I had the special good fortune to be present in the audience at the Conference of the United Nations on June 26, 1945, in San Francisco! It was a sunny California morning. Excitement filled the air, for on this day the United Nations Charter was to be signed in the San Francisco Memorial Opera House. It was a day of worldwide interest and anticipation. People crowded the sidewalk to see representatives of fifty nations, including President Harry S. Truman, enter the Opera House foyer.

The setting on the stage was most unusual. On the curtain at the back was a large gold seal of the United Nations, and in a semicircle on the stage were the faintly waving flags of many, many nations. President Truman presided at the conference and was seated at a large oval table. After addresses were made by several important statesmen, the time came for the signing of the Charter. Then, in the most thrilling moment of the conference, a flag was brought onto the stage: the flag of the United Nations. To my great astonishment I saw the fulfillment of prophecy. The wish of 'Abdu'l-Bahá had come true; the flag of international peace was unfurled in California. On this unforgettable occasion *The Bahá'í Peace Program* booklet was presented to every person attending the conference.

Part 3

After 'Abdu'l-Bahá Returned to Haifa

After 'Abdu'l-Bahá Returned to Haifa

We knew that the California Bahá'ís had not been forgotten by 'Abdu'l-Bahá upon His return to Haifa. Juanita Storch, one of the "Peach Tree" group, received a Tablet from the Master written October 22, 1916, a portion of which said:

> Convey on My behalf the utmost kindness to the friends of God and the maidservants of the Merciful, and say to them: "Ye are the young incomparable trees of the garden of the love of God. Strive ye so that ye may produce luscious fruits. Ye are the green plants of the meadow of the Kingdom; I hope that, through the downpouring of the rain of the heavenly grace, ye may ever remain fresh, verdant, and tender. While I was staying in California, I observed that that pure ground has infinite capacity. Like unto the farmer, I scattered seeds. Now I hope that the field has become green, its tall stalks waving in the breeze; in due season many great and rich harvests be gathered, and day by day greater progress be obtained.

Dr. F. W. D'Evelyn, a learned and very firm Bahá'í, was another of the early believers in San Francisco. In a Tablet dated April 21, 1914, from Haifa, 'Abdu'l-Bahá encouraged Dr. D'Evelyn and a few others to plan the first International Bahá'í Conference in 1915:

> To Doctor F. W. D'Evelyn, the beloved of God, Mrs. Helen S. Goodall, the maid-servant of God, Mrs. Ella

G. Cooper, Mr. W. C. and Mrs. Georgia Ralston, San Francisco, California.

Upon them be BAHA'O'LLAH-EL-ABHA!
HE IS GOD!

O ye who are firm in the Covenant!
Your letter was received. Praise be to God, that with the utmost firmness you have arisen in the service of the Kingdom, so that you may organize a Congress for universal peace during the Panama-Pacific International Exposition. Summon the people to the Kingdom of God and promote the teachings of His Holiness BAHA'O'LLAH. Rest ye assured that the Divine Confirmations will be conducive to joy and fragrance and most great results will be the outcome of this service.

Rest ye confident in the assistance of God.
Upon ye be Baha-El-ABHA!
(Signed) ABDUL-BAHA ABBAS.[1]

In another Tablet to the women of the California Bahá'í community 'Abdu'l-Bahá wrote:

If you arise in accord with the exhortations and commands of the Blessed Perfection—may my life be a sacrifice to His beloved ones!—before long agreeable results will be obtained, the great newspapers of the world will all engage in praising you and such activity will be brought about in the West as will increase the motion and activity in the East.[2]

Often I remember these words of the Master when I read in American newspapers and magazines announcements of proclamation meetings and articles about the Faith, hear interviews with Bahá'í speakers on television and radio, and in foreign newspapers and magazines see photographs of Bahá'í traveling teachers and stories about Bahá'í activities around the world.

Five years after 'Abdu'l-Bahá returned to Haifa, the American and Canadian Bahá'ís received His Tablets of the Divine Plan. These Tablets [which outlined the international teaching mission of the Bahá'ís of the United States and Canada] were read in a meeting attended by Martha Root, one of the very early believers. Martha left the gathering; when a friend went to look for her, he found her in her room packing her suitcase.

Shoghi Effendi said of her: "To Martha Root, that archetype of Bahá'í itinerant teachers and the foremost Hand raised by Bahá'u'lláh since 'Abdu'l-Bahá's passing, must be awarded, if her manifold services and the supreme act of her life are to be correctly appraised, the title of Leading Ambassadress of His Faith and Pride of Bahá'í teachers, whether men or women, in both the East and the West." Martha, he continued, "established a record that constitutes the nearest approach to the example set by 'Abdu'l-Bahá Himself . . . in the course of His journeys throughout the West."[3] It was through her sweet and gentle teaching that Queen Marie of Rumania became a follower of Bahá'u'lláh. Martha passed away September 28, 1939, in Honolulu. Friends from all over the world now visit her grave and pray there.

Agnes Alexander, also later to be named a Hand of the Cause of God, and the only one to be mentioned in the Tablets of the Divine Plan, was another of the early believers. She was called by 'Abdu'l-Bahá "the daughter of the Kingdom" and "the beloved maid-servant of the Blessed Perfection."[4] On August 21, 1914, she received approval from the Master of her plan to go to Japan to teach the Faith. He wrote: "thy voyage to Japan is preferred to everything else."[5] On that day she was in Switzerland; her money was in England; and her luggage, in Germany. Despite the perils of war she left immediately. Martha Root joined her in Japan several times, and together they traveled throughout that country, teaching the Faith constantly. They then went to Korea and to the mainland of China. Later, alone, Agnes went to Taiwan and to the Philippines.

Agnes was the first Bahá'í pioneer to Japan who became a resident of Japan. I met Agnes in Berkeley in 1915, while she was visiting her sister, and we formed a lasting friendship. Often, to our astonishment and delight, we met unexpectedly in many places in the world. Throughout our years of friendship we kept in touch by correspondence. Agnes wrote me from Tokyo in June 1959 that she had attended the yearly meeting of the "All Blind" at the Prefectural School for the Blind in Kyoto, where Mr. Tokujiro Torii, a Bahá'í, was vice-principal. She said that she was invited to speak at that meeting—but for only "one minute." Mr. Torii translated for Agnes when she was called upon to speak, and four hundred blind people, who had gathered from different parts of Japan, heard for the first time the word *Bahá'í*. She said: "Mr. Torii is my friend. I have known him for forty years. I am a Bahá'í." Then she mentioned the social principles of Bahá'u'lláh, her "minute" was over, and she sat down. Agnes wrote that there was much confusion in the room and flashing of lights, and she wondered why. The next morning, to her utter amazement, she saw in the newspaper her picture and an article about the Bahá'í Faith. Unknown to her, she had been seen on television and heard on radio throughout Japan.

Mr. Torii was sent on a trip to Rome by the Prefectural School for the Blind in September 1954, and it was there that I met him. He had received an invitation from Shoghi Effendi to make a pilgrimage, but Mr. Torii's aide and companion could not accompany him because of his religious belief, so the pilgrimage was not made. We all shared Mr. Torii's disappointment.[6]

Agnes was in Paris in September 1959. She wrote to me in Salzburg, where I was pioneering, asking me to meet her in Frankfurt in October and accompany her to Rome. I cabled her that I would be able to do so. While we were flying to Rome, Agnes told me that it was in the spring of 1900, when she was staying in a pension in Rome, that she met Mrs. Dixon and her two daughters. They were returning to their home in the United States after a pilgrimage to meet 'Abdu'l-Bahá in 'Akká. One day Agnes heard Mrs. Dixon conversing with a lady in the elevator about 'Abdu'l-Bahá. Later, Agnes asked Mrs. Dixon if she would tell her, too, about 'Abdu'l-Bahá. Mrs.

Dixon then invited her to her room and told her about 'Abdu'l-Bahá and the Bahá'í Faith. Agnes said: "My heart was touched, and I told Mrs. Dixon that I knew Christ was on the earth." Mrs. Dixon arranged for Agnes to correspond with May Bolles, and Agnes met May in Paris in 1901. Agnes said, "That meeting was one of the most precious memories of my life." Their friendship continued all of their lives.

One of my fondest memories of Agnes is the day we arrived in Rome, October 26, 1959. It was the fifty-ninth anniversary of that day when she had first heard of the Faith of Bahá'u'lláh, and she wanted me to be with her. She told me that this was her first return to her "spiritual home," as she called Rome. I had never seen her so joyous. As we walked away from the plane, she said, "Dear, it is so wonderful to have you here with me. You are my spiritual sister, and I love you very much. I am very happy that we are together on my spiritual birthday." Hands of the Cause of God—Amelia Collins, John Ferraby, and Ugo Giachery were in Rome; and Dr. Giachery came to greet her at the plane. After spending several wonderful days with the friends in Rome, the Hands proceeded to a meeting in Haifa, and I returned to Salzburg.

Agnes wrote to me on March 7, 1962, and enclosed a very unusual picture from Kyoto, Japan:

> Now is a new time, I feel definitely, and the Cause will spread more. I am enclosing a photo of the first of the Ainu people, the aborigines of Japan who live in the Northern island of Japan, to accept the Faith. They were guests in Kobe for eight days in one of the Persian homes. They all wear long beards, but the younger one, second from my right, cut his off as his sacrifice when he became a Bahá'í. He said he had nothing worthwhile to give and he loved his long black beard the most of all, so that was his sacrifice.
>
> Thank you, darling Ramona, for your prayers for me. We have to learn to depend on God alone and He will never fail us.   Always your loving Agnes

Agnes Alexander's outstanding qualities were complete trust in God's will, strict obedience and loyalty to the Master's Will and Testament, and the sweet, pure, gentle spirit with which she taught. She was audacious and persevering in whatever she set out to accomplish. In Tokyo she suffered an accident on July 28, 1965. Her family in Honolulu begged her to come to Hawaii, but she refused, saying that she preferred to remain in the Japanese hospital where she had opportunities to speak of the Faith to Japanese people. After two years she returned to Kyoto on July 7, 1967, for a short time, and then moved to Honolulu to spend her remaining years in the Arcadia, a lovely senior citizens' home near the site of her parents' home, where she was born. Agnes and I continued to correspond until shortly before her death on January 1, 1971; at nearly ninety-six years of age, she was the oldest living Hand of the Cause of God at that time. During the years at the Arcadia friends visited her from all over the world, and she continued to teach until the end of her life.

'Abdu'l-Bahá wrote in the Tablets of the Divine Plan, recalling His visit to California: "Particularly was I greatly pleased with the meetings in San Francisco and Oakland, the gatherings in Los Angeles, and the believers who came from the cities of other states. Whenever their faces cross My memory, immediately infinite happiness is realized."[7]

In subsequent years a number of Californians went to the Holy Land on pilgrimage. Among them were John and Louise Bosch. John, a native of Switzerland, was one of the first believers in California. His sweetheart, Louise, also Swiss, came to America as a young woman and became a Bahá'í in the East. They corresponded for a time; then, at John's request, she came to San Francisco. They were often in our home during their courtship. She fascinated me with her delightful European appearance and the Swiss accent, which she never lost.

Shortly after Louise arrived in California, they were married and went to live in Geyserville. From there, they attended meetings in Oakland, which was quite a distance away. John was superintendent of two wineries in northern California. Because of Bahá'u'lláh's law prohibiting the drinking of alcohol, John eventually gave up his position and planted his own land in the wine country with diversified crops. Later on the Bosches offered the use of their Geyserville property as the first Bahá'í summer school in the West. From this school the Faith was spread far and wide by many teachers and students who traveled long distances to attend classes under the "Big Tree" and in Collins Hall.

In 1920, in response to the Tablets of the Divine Plan, the Bosches took the Faith of Bahá'u'lláh to Tahiti. They were in Haifa at the time of the death of 'Abdu'l-Bahá in 1921. After many years of service John died on July 22, 1946, and Louise followed on September 6, 1952. Both are buried in Geyserville.

In 1920 four dedicated and steadfast California believers—Helen Goodall, Ella Cooper, Kathryn Frankland, and Georgia Ralston—were invited by the Master to visit Him in Haifa. After their pilgrimage [of thirty days] 'Abdu'l-Bahá said of the pilgrims in a talk to His family and friends in His home in Haifa on November 25, 1920:

> The friends who departed recently, that is, the friends from America, Mrs. Goodall, Mrs. Cooper, Mrs. Ralston, Mrs. Frankland, and from France, Mr. and Mrs. Dreyfus, have determined to strive to promote and spread the Word of God with all their energy. They have confined all their thoughts to this excellent intention. . . . They departed from here with utmost sincerity of purpose and devotion to Bahá'u'lláh. The truth of this statement was not so well known while they were here; but after they return home, this will become manifest, and you will hear what they will achieve. Now you should pray for them and supplicate confirmation and assistance for them that they may be able to promote the Word of God and be favored with the privilege of serving the world of humanity, that they may help to establish universal peace and lay the

foundation of the oneness of the world of humanity. They should be kind to all people and prefer the welfare of others to their own. When they attain to these characteristics, the Hosts of the Supreme Concourse will assist them, and the confirmations of the Kingdom of Abha will surround them. Every one of them will become a brilliant candle and a victorious banner, not only they themselves, but others will become astonished; but they are in need of your prayers. Whenever you are supplicating ask confirmations for them.

Today every soul who gives up his own thoughts and desires and mingles with the people with utmost sincerity, such an one is surrounded by the Hosts of the Supreme Concourse: as a magnet attracts iron these benevolent intentions similarly attract the divine confirmations. You shall see before long that every one of the friends will be confirmed to achieve distinguished services. Do not think that he or she is weak or without fame; consider his characteristics, his sincerity, truthfulness, willingness to serve, trustworthiness, etc., not his position in society. Such a person is confirmed, otherwise all the doors of confirmation will be closed.

Therefore, you should supplicate and pray for such friends as these and implore confirmations and assistance.[8]

Kathryn Frankland was a tiny, delicate woman, but energetic, self-sacrificing, and strong in her faith. I met Kathryn in 1906 when we attended the meetings in Helen Goodall's home, and we enjoyed a close friendship for many years. She and her husband, Alec, moved to Berkeley about 1916, and they held many meetings in their home.[9] For several years she also conducted children's classes where our children were taught about the Faith. It was there that I met 'Alí Yazdí, a member of the well-known family of Muḥammad-'Alí Ṣabbáq of Yazd, mentioned in *Memorials of the Faithful*, who was exiled to Turkey with Bahá'u'lláh, assisted the believers in Constantinople as they came and went through that city on their way to meet Bahá'u'lláh in Adrianople, and at one time welcomed and helped the early pilgrims who arrived at 'Akká in ships.[10] 'Alí and his wife, Marion, have upheld the teaching work in Berkeley for many years.

Kathryn had the gift of making people feel happy and welcome wherever she lived. Sometimes she would invite people she met casually to have tea with her, and she would tell them about the Faith. Kathryn was a friendly, gay little person, and everyone felt her warmth and love for humanity. She was often in the hospital; because her bones were very brittle, she suffered several fractures. Kathryn used these occasions to teach the Faith to her doctors and others who attended her. She was never unhappy over these vicissitudes. She told me, "God gave me these opportunities to teach the Faith."

On one of our last visits together Kathryn gave me a linen handkerchief, which had belonged to 'Abdu'l-Bahá, and four Bahá'í ringstones given to her by the Greatest Holy Leaf during her pilgrimage in 1920. She was always generous and sweet, sharing her vast knowledge of the Teachings and her worldly possessions.

When Kathryn was in Haifa, 'Abdu'l-Bahá gave her a message for my mother:

> Give her my kindest greeting, and to her son, and to the wife of her son, to her daugher and her husband, and to her grandchildren. Give them my loving greetings.
>
> I pray for them that they will be assisted in the service of the Kingdom and will have physical success in this world.
>
> For Dr. Woodson Allen from the Merciful God I ask His forgiveness at the time of his departure because the last word he uttered was the Greatest Name; it [this Word] had great effect in the Kingdom of Abhá. Therefore, Dr. Allen must be sure that his children will be assisted.

After Kathryn's pilgrimage, she pioneered in many cities in the United States. She returned to Berkeley for a short period [during which she helped to establish the first

Spiritual Assembly of Berkeley in 1925]. Later she moved to Riverside, California, where many opportunities and doors opened for her. In 1957 she was in Chula Vista when I was pioneering in Salzburg. We made plans to meet and make a pilgrimage to Haifa in December 1957, but these were altered because of the passing of Shoghi Effendi. I was never with Kathryn again after our last meeting in 1953 at the dedication of the Bahá'í House of Worship in Wilmette. Shortly before her death, Kathryn moved to Oakland, where she passed away November 4, 1963. She is buried next to her husband in the Sunset Cemetery in Berkeley. Since her passing, I have felt a deep personal loss; for she had always been a precious part of my Bahá'í life.

To Helen Goodall, on her last visit to Haifa in 1920, the Master said: "I desire for you a new confirmation at every moment and wish for you the wonderful providence and assistance so that the city of San Francisco may become a lamp and you the light shining through it." Shoghi Effendi expressed his admiration for Helen when he referred to her as "the one who conferred distinction on the generation to which she belonged." Helen passed away February 19, 1922, in San Francisco. 'Abdu'l-Bahá once said that the Goodall home in Oakland would be a place of pilgrimage. Indeed it was, while it stood; and now, even though a modern apartment building has replaced it, friends still visit that spot and pray there.

In the mid-1920s the Oakland Spiritual Assembly lapsed for several years. Then, through the efforts of Orcella Rexford and the dedicated long-time Bahá'í, Leroy Ioas, later named a Hand of the Cause, a number of new believers entered the Faith. One of the most devoted and united families in the Bay Area—John and Annie Linfoot, their daughters, Charlotte and Gladys, and their son, William—were among this group. Mrs. Linfoot was a most active Bahá'í; and Mr. Linfoot and William worked diligently for several years at Geyserville School to make the grounds and buildings a beautiful place for young and old alike to enjoy. In 1954 Charlotte moved to Wilmette, where she has served for many years as [assistant] secretary of the National Spiritual Assembly, and Gladys has worked for several national committees. Charlotte is known and loved throughout the Bahá'í world for her purity of spirit, her knowledge of the Teachings, and her loving interest in the many friends she has made during long years of faithful service. Surely the spiritual unity of the Linfoot family was the cause of great bounty to them and to the Faith.[11]

Throughout the years Ella Cooper continued actively to serve the Cause. She often made arrangements to present outstanding Bahá'í speakers at large civic affairs, before clubs, and at Bahá'í Congresses held in San Francisco. During the Pan American International Exposition of 1915 she planned for Bahá'í speakers to present the Faith to the public. She attended the National Bahá'í Conventions in Wilmette and was instrumental in arranging the First Western Conference in San Francisco, held on November 24-26, 1922, for the purpose of finding ways to carry on the Word and spread the Teachings more effectively. Ella was a member of the National Spiritual Assembly for two years and a member of the Local Assembly in San Francisco from 1921 until 1934.

One of my most poignant memories of Ella is the day I saw her in San Francisco, after a luncheon at the Women's City Club, walking to where she could take a trolley car back to her home. Because of the gasoline shortage during World War II, she had dispensed with her car and chauffeur, and in order to do her share in conserving gasoline, she refused to take a taxi. This act was typical of Ella and an insight into her character.

Through the years Ella and I spent many happy hours together. Often she invited me to her home for lunch and a visit. In the springtime she enjoyed driving down the Peninsula to a violet farm where she had a large wicker basket filled with bunches of dark purple violets for me. Their exquisite fragrance permeated the car as we drove along the ocean. Later, Ella's chauffeur, Henry Keeling, a Bahá'í, would drive us back to San Francisco, drop her off at home, then drive me to my house in Berkeley where I would share the violets with my friends.

With elegance and dignity, Ella maintained a home in San Francisco for her husband, Charles, and her brother, Arthur. All of her life she enjoyed the love and respect of a circle of social friends. Never did she lose an opportunity to serve the Cause to her fullest capacity. She held meetings in her home and always wanted one of the "Peaches" to be present. Bahá'ís from all over the world came to visit Ella, to enjoy her hospitality and receive their portion of her loving kindness and knowledge of the Teachings. Ella enjoyed entertaining small groups for tea. From her living room we could look through large glass windows at colorful San Francisco Bay and see the ships passing under the Golden Gate Bridge, and in the springtime see the hills blazing with golden California poppies.

One afternoon Marion Little, one of the outstanding early pioneers to Europe, Katherine Baldwin, one of the first believers in Honolulu, and I were guests at Ella's. After tea was served, Ella told stories about 'Abdu'l-Bahá and her pilgrimages to see Him, and about the early days of the Faith. Her radiant face was lovely to look upon as she spoke. Then prayers were read. The room of this gracious lady's home seemed filled with the presence of the Master. That afternoon we were so happy that we lost all sense of time, until suddenly we saw the sun slipping into the Golden Gate, casting a golden rosy glow over the city that had been so blessed by the presence and spirit of 'Abdu'l-Bahá. We knew it was time for us to leave, our hearts filled with love for "Aunt Ella."

As the years passed, Ella's pretty brown hair turned silvery white, and she used tiny silver hairpins to hold it in place. She was a dainty lady, always beautifully groomed. She kept her youthful spirit and graciously accepted the changes taking place, especially in the lives of the young friends whom she had taught. Her loving interest in my children has had a lasting influence on their lives, and she was overjoyed when she became "Grandmother Peach" to Barbara's daughter "Bobbin," as she named her. Despite her frail health and loss of vigor, Ella served the Cause she loved so well until she passed away on July 12, 1951.

In 1922 my mother, in answer to an invitation from 'Abdu'l-Bahá, had planned to make a pilgrimage with a friend, Helen Whitney, who later married Lou Eggleston (the Egglestons donated the property for the Bahá'í School in Davison, Michigan, to the Faith). However, the following Tablet, dated October 6, 1921, was received by my mother shortly before the Master passed to the Abhá Kingdom:

> Through Mr. Latimer, Mrs. Frances Allen; upon her be the Glory of God the Most Glorious,
>
> He is God.
> O thou who are firm in the Covenant!
> Thy letter has been received. From the Kingdom of Abhá I ask assistance and bestowal for all the members of thy family, so that it might bless them all.
> His Honor Fazel breathed the spirit of life in America. You must rear the souls. Thou art permitted to come, but next year. Engage now in Teaching. Owing to the lack of time, I am writing briefly. Thou shouldst pardon that.
> Upon thee be the Glory of Abhá.
>
> abdul Bahá abbas

When my mother received this, we became aware that our beloved 'Abdu'l-Bahá was overburdened and that His strength was gradually leaving Him. This made us sad. I recalled His activities during His stay in the San Francisco Bay Area, the meetings where He had spoken to hundreds of people, the private interviews He had held with eminent people, humble people, and the people of different races and creeds, who had flocked to Him for answers to their many and varied questions and to have the bounty of being in His presence and of receiving their portion of His love. I remembered His visits to several cities in California, where He spoke and met with the friends, constantly looking into new faces, finding Himself in strange surroundings. It was no surprise to me that the Master was always at ease when meeting people, whether of great distinction or of the most lowly station; for He treated all alike, with love, kindness, and courtesy. He showed great tenderness and compassion to the poor. To me it was astonishing that He so easily accustomed Himself to the different manner of living, to the noise and bustle of the large cities with all their bright lights, and to the mixed audiences of men and women, as though these had always been a part of His life. There were moments when He showed the effect of His years of imprisonment and deprivation, and I was unhappy and sorry because I knew that this was the result of His years of suffering for mankind.

Toward the end of 'Abdu'l-Bahá's visit in California He appeared sometimes to be sad because of the failure of many people to respond to His call to humanity, to accept the glorious Teachings of Bahá'u'lláh. Lua told me that when she heard the Master chant the Visitation Tablet, at the stanza "Waft, then, unto me, O my God and my Beloved . . . the holy breaths of Thy favors, that they may draw me away from myself and from the world. . . . ," He seemed to be pleading so earnestly with Bahá'u'lláh to release Him from this world that it broke her heart, and she would weep and weep.[12]

On November 29, 1921, I was walking with my little daughter and my young son along a country road near our home in Berkeley; Barbara suddenly stopped and said, "Look, Mommy, there is 'Abdu'l-Bahá walking with your daddy in front of us!" I said, "I think you are mistaken," but she said, "No, no, there is 'Abdu'l-Bahá walking with your daddy in front of us!" Then I explained to her that the Master was in this world, in Haifa, but my father was in another world, so she could not see them together. However, she kept insisting they were walking arm in arm in front of us, and I said nothing more. The next day, in a letter from Ella Cooper, came the grievous news that on November 28 our beloved 'Abdu'l-Bahá had winged His flight from this world to the Abhá Kingdom.

MARTHA ROOT
Hand of the Cause of God and called by Shoghi Effendi the
"Leading Ambassadress of His Faith."

JOHN and LOUISE BOSCH
gave land for the site of the Bahá'í school
at Geyserville, California.

MARK TOBEY and KATHRYN FRANKLAND
at a Bahá'í convention in Wilmette, Illinois.

BAHÁ'Í CHILDREN'S CLASS
taught by Kathryn Frankland in Berkeley, California,
in the early days.

Front row, left to right: Nephew of Ella Cooper (holding child), unknown, niece of Ella Cooper, and Barbara Bray.

Back row, left to right: Niece of Ella Cooper (in hat), niece of Ella Cooper, Helen Frankland (with hairbow, daughter of Kathryn), niece of Ella Cooper, (child) Allen Bray, and Lorne Mattesen.

photograph courtesy Ramona Brown

'ABDU'L-BAHÁ
and friends, including the pilgrims from California in 1920, shown in front of the Shrine of the Báb on Mt. Carmel.
Front row, seated, left to right of 'Abdu'l-Bahá:
  Emogene Hoagg, Georgia Ralston, Helen Goodall, Julie Culver, Ella Cooper, Kathryn Frankland.
Back row: Saichiro Fujita (back of Ella Cooper).

The news was heartbreaking to those of us who had been blessed by His loving-kindness, who had stood before Him and looked into His wonderful eyes, and who had been privileged to receive His guidance for so many years. Our hearts were saddened, and we wept because of the separation from our beloved Master. Then came the realization that He had at last attained His heart's desire—to be in the Kingdom of God! He was free of the burdens He had borne all of His life, and we knew we should be happy for Him. Less than six months before His passing, 'Abdu'l-Bahá revealed this prayer in honor of a kinsman of the Báb: "O Lord, My Lord! Hasten My ascension unto Thy sublime Threshold . . . and My arrival at the Door of Thy grace beneath the shadow of Thy most great mercy . . ."[13]

Soon after the ascension of the Master, we learned that He had not left us without someone to guide us and to protect the Faith; for He had written His Will and Testament in which He appointed His grandson Shoghi Effendi the Guardian, to whom we all should turn. In a short time Ella Cooper provided each one of us with a typewritten copy of the document that is the foundation of the Administrative Order.

Shoghi Effendi led us on paths of endeavor and accomplishment which the early believers never dreamed would take place in this century. When he died suddenly on November 4, 1957, the shocking and sad news affected the whole world; for he had been a "true brother" [the term he used in closing many of his letters] to the Bahá'ís everywhere. For a time the world seemed empty. However, the Guardian, like 'Abdu'l-Bahá, had given us our work and tasks to do; and our greatest, loving tribute to him has been to carry forward his systematic program for the spread of the Faith throughout the world.

As I gaze out of my window at the blue Pacific Ocean, I remember 'Abdu'l-Bahá's words in the *Tablets of the Divine Plan*:

> The blessed state of California bears the utmost similarity to the Holy Land, that is, the country of

Palestine. . . . Even the shores of the Pacific Ocean, in some instances, show perfect resemblance to the shores of the Holy Land. . . .

Now California and the other Western States must earn an ideal similarity with the Holy Land, and from that state and that region the breaths of the Holy Spirit be diffused to all parts of America and Europe. . . .[14]

From the home of Helen Goodall and Ella Cooper the Teachings of Bahá'u'lláh spread, and Bahá'í communities sprang up in many parts of California. From their inspiring lives and their efforts, pioneers went out into the world during the years following the revelation of the Tablets of the Divine Plan, then during the Seven Year Plans and the Ten Year Crusade. Many who had been nurtured by these wonderful women left their homes to go to Europe, Australia, Africa, and other places.

In *God Passes By*, his masterpiece on the history of the Bahá'í Faith, the Guardian stated:

> The establishment of the Faith of Bahá'u'lláh in the Western Hemisphere—the most outstanding achievement that will forever be associated with 'Abdu'l-Bahá's ministry—had . . . set in motion such tremendous forces, and been productive of such far-reaching results, as to warrant the active and personal participation of the Center of the Covenant Himself in those epoch-making activities which His Western disciples had, through the propelling power of that Covenant, boldly initiated and were vigorously prosecuting.
>
> . . . He arose with sublime courage, confidence and resolution to consecrate what little strength remained to Him, in the evening of His life, to a service of such heroic proportions that no parallel to it is to be found in the annals of the first Bahá'í century.[15]

A fleeting moment of sadness comes over me as I remember the moment of parting with our beloved Master. It was in the afternoon of October 26, 1912, that He left Sacramento to visit several cities on His way back to New York and then to Haifa. As usual He was traveling in the most modest way, riding and sleeping in a chair car. He said: "We are the army of God; we deny ourselves luxury or comfort as all armies do." It was a heartbreaking day for us who had been blessed by the bounty of His presence. 'Abdu'l-Bahá did not wish a large gathering at the railroad station when He left, but Ella Cooper and a few of us were permitted to see Him depart and to wave farewell. I wondered what His thoughts were as He looked out of the window at His little group of dedicated followers.

My cup had been filled to overflowing, and I knew then that the Master's wish was for all of us to share with others the love He had showered upon us. He had given us great bounties and great responsibilities. My last glimpse of His beloved face was through the window of the coach with the shades partly drawn; as the train slowly started, He smiled sweetly and a little wistfully as He looked out at us and very gently waved His hand.

We stood silently a moment, each with his own feeling of sadness and loss, but aware that we would never be separated from the spiritual nearness of 'Abdu'l-Bahá, for He had said, "My presence will be with you always."

Impart thou the Greatest Name to the ears, so that all may call out among nations: "O Thou Baha' of the world! O Thou Sun of Pre-existence!"

Truly, I say unto thee, this blessed Name is the spirit of life, the deliverer from death, the word of salvation and of manifest signs! Thou shalt surely hear from all parts the cry, "Ya Baha EL-ABHA!" reaching to the Supreme Concourse.

'Abdu'l-Bahá[16]

Part 4

Coda

Coda

In 1946 my husband, Arthur Brown, and I moved into a new home in Oakland. Shortly afterwards Agnes Alexander spoke at our first meeting, and on that day Arthur and I dedicated our home to the service of Bahá'u'lláh. Many Bahá'í activities took place in our home; friends enjoyed the meetings where Ella Cooper, Mark Tobey, Marzieh Gail, Bahia Gulick, Loulie Mathews, and many others spoke. It was from this home, after the passing of Arthur, that my daughter [Barbara], my granddaughter ["Bobbin"], and I attended the dedication of the Bahá'í House of Worship in Wilmette in 1953. After this I went to the Intercontinental Conference in Stockholm, Sweden, and visited the Bahá'ís of Oslo and Copenhagen for several months before returning to my home in Oakland in December. My deep desire was to arrange my affairs quickly and go pioneering. However, to my surprise and joy, I received an invitation to make my pilgrimage in May, and I deferred my other plans.

It was early afternoon on May 10, 1954, when I arrived in Haifa. As my taxi approached the Eastern Pilgrim House, suddenly through the treetops I caught a glimpse of the golden dome of the Shrine of the Báb. Never will I forget the exhilaration of that moment! After my first outburst of joy, I was silent. Other fleeting views of the Shrine appeared, but I was too overcome to utter a sound. Arriving at the Western Pilgrim House where we were to stay, I was greeted by Jessie Revell, who told me that she would accompany me to the house of 'Abdu'l-

Bahá where I had been invited to have tea with Rúḥíyyih Khánum. As I walked up the steps, I was thrilled by the thought that the Master had for years climbed these same steps, and I entered the large main room where He had so often received His guests. As Rúḥíyyih Khánum came toward me with outstretched arms and lovingly embraced me, I could feel the very presence of 'Abdu'l-Bahá. Later I was able to spend some time alone in prayer and meditation at the side of the iron bed in the modest room nearby where the Master had slept and passed away in 1921.

Soon it was the dinner hour at the Western Pilgrim House, and my dream of being in the presence of our beloved Guardian was coming true. Shoghi Effendi and Rúḥíyyih Khánum had already entered the dining room. I stood with the group of friends outside the dining room waiting for others to go in. They said to me, "Go on in. Go in!" but I hesitated. Then I was gently pushed by Milly Collins into the room. There I saw him—"The sign of God," the "priceless pearl!"[1] My heart stood still. I could not speak or move until he came toward me smiling and took my hand, saying, "Welcome, Mrs. Brown. We are very happy to see you and have you with us. Please sit here"; he indicated a chair opposite him at the dinner table. The warmth of his greeting and his gentle courtesy made me feel comfortable and happy. I sensed his quiet, deep, spiritual strength. Shoghi Effendi asked me about my daughter. He looked a long time at the pictures of my family, and I gave him the message each one had sent him. Then he looked at me, smiled, and said, "How is your son, Mrs. Brown?" I replied that Allen had sent him his greetings and a special message, which I relayed to him. He said, "Tell your son that I hope his wishes to serve and help will be gratified." Looking again at the photographs, the Guardian said that he would pray in the Holy Shrines for my family.

Then in a gentle and loving manner he inquired about the believers in California and spoke of some of the early Bahá'ís whom I had known—Helen Goodall, Ella Cooper, Phoebe Hearst, and Lua Getsinger. Often as we sat with Shoghi Effendi he seemed to know what was in our hearts, for he answered questions that were in my own heart but which I had not asked.

In the morning of the second day at Bahjí I went with Mary and Alan Elston, two pioneers from Africa, and [the gardener] Sala to pray in the Shrine of Bahá'u'lláh. To enter the Shrine one passes through a beautiful, small, wrought-iron gate and steps on a short path of white pebbles leading to the handsome bronze door of the Shrine. On either side of the path is a pillar. I put my hand on the ledge of a pillar to steady myself as I removed my shoes before entering the Shrine, and my hand fell upon three glorious white carnations! I was surprised and exclaimed over them because I had not seen any carnations in the gardens. I was deeply touched when Sala said, "Shoghi Effendi put them there yesterday when he visited the Shrine, and I am sure that he meant them for you!" When Sala said this, I wondered whether Shoghi Effendi knew that carnations have a special significance to me and are very dear to my heart. I remembered that Zikr'u'lláh Khadem, a Hand of the Cause of God, had once said to me, "The beloved Guardian knows the heart of each one of us."

Each evening at dinner Shoghi Effendi wore a light tan camel's hair overcoat, a white shirt, and a black tie. His complexion was a soft tan and his large brown eyes expressed his every emotion. From under his black fez, on each side, a few white hairs were mingled with the black. He was not a large man, but his presence filled the room. When the Guardian spoke of the accomplishments of the Bahá'ís the world over, he never included himself. He was a humble, gentle person and generally spoke in a soft voice; but when he explained the Administration, he spoke with a firm tone and great authority. When he was not speaking in a serious vein, he often made us laugh as he related some funny incident or experience that he or someone else had had, and then his eyes twinkled as he laughed. Nothing made Shoghi Effendi happier than news of the unity among the believers. During dinner he often spoke of what was occurring in many parts of the world. Some evenings he would stay after dinner was over and tell us of good news he had received or explain some special Teaching.

Each evening after the Guardian had left the dining room, Rúḥíyyih Khánum and we three pilgrims would visit in the sitting room, and she would tell us of some special news or incident that had made Shoghi Effendi very happy. After she left, we would recall the words of the Guardian and later compare our notes. One evening Shoghi Effendi said, "Please share your notes that you have taken here with the friends when you return home." This I have tried to do ever since, and following are some of the important and interesting things which he said to us while we were his guests in Haifa:

> Bahá'ís must have a new way of life. They need to be different from other people. They must be distinguished. The more distinguished, the more they will attract people. The greater the distinction, the greater the attraction. They must read the Tablets of 'Abdu'l-Bahá, study the text of the Teachings. It is not enough to be good and kind and to lead a religious life today; it does not count for much unless one accepts the Manifestation of God, if one has heard of Him; it is almost wasted. One must accept the Manifestation in His day. If one has not heard of Bahá'u'lláh, they are not to blame; the blame lies with the Bahá'ís. If the Bahá'ís fail to teach the Faith, the people who do not hear of the Faith are not to blame. The blame lies with the Bahá'ís.

> All men are not of the same capacity. To serve to full capacity is meritorious with God. God judges men by how they use their capacity.

> Every city, every town, and every village will have a [Bahá'í] Temple and a House of Justice in the future.

There are three processes in teaching: the first is to attract the people; the second is to convert the people; and the third is to be consecrated. There must be attraction, conversion, and consecration. The teachers must not be unwise. There are three Charters to be used: (1) the Covenant of Bahá'u'lláh, or the Divine Plan; (2) the Will and Testament of 'Abdu'l-Bahá with the plan for world administration; and (3) the Tablet of Carmel, the Charter for the development for the World Center of the Faith.[2] The Tablet of Carmel is the symbol of the House of Justice. The Ark is the symbol of the Administrative Body. The higher cave of Elijah is the real one where Bahá'u'lláh revealed the Tablet of Carmel in such a loud voice that the priests heard it.

It is essential that the youth of today study deeply the Faith as they will usher in the Most Great Peace. The Lesser Peace will be established within this century. The Most Great Peace in the next century. The Global Crusade will establish the Bahá'í Faith the world over but will not have a direct influence in establishing the United States of the World. The first period will be that of suffering and cleansing; the second period will be that of unification; and the third, the establishment of the Bahá'í World Faith. After the International State is established and wars cease, the money now being expended for destruction and war will be used for education and science, and a method will be discovered for interplanetary communication, even interplanetary conferences. The time will come when people can cross the entire nation in one hour and eventually beyond the continent into interplanetary travel. The cycle of six thousand years of city building has come to an end, and now we will have a new pattern starting with villages, etc. Material civilization is becoming like the ancient city of Babylon, and it must be destroyed.

The young people must disperse far away, the old

ones to outlying places; they must settle goal cities. Sell your property and pioneer! . . . The young people of America should go out into the country on farms and work with their hands and produce food for their families.

Americans are exposed to great dangers. Today the power of America is in the hands of the masses.[3] There is a terrific power in the press, and the people are swayed by it. The United States, on a national scale, sets the pattern for an international pattern. . . . There will be a world civil war followed by the establishment of a world state; all the nations will be a part of it and will have to conform to it. This war has already started in Korea. Mankind cannot be purified and cleansed without suffering. . . . It is positively dangerous to live in cities. The cities are doomed. They will go up in smoke. They will evaporate. . . . The Bahá'ís must disperse from the cities. . . . Why do they not disperse? If they do not respond and disperse, they will suffer spiritually, materially, and physically. . . . In America the destruction will be great! . . . They must disperse for their own protection. The cities are doomed: New York, Chicago, San Francisco, Los Angeles. They must flee from the United States because America will become the storm center of the future. . . . Buy property in Central Africa! Those with independent means must pack up and go. . . . Those with spirit must pack up and go. . . . There must be a mass response. . . . I can warn them, but I cannot make them go. . . . The Cause will triumph in spite of the actions and inactivity of the believers. If one country falls down, another will make up for it. The Bahá'ís have been given the method. Now they must have the spirit. It is hopeless for capable teachers in the cities (the people will not listen). . . . The friends are calculating too much, and there is too much emphasis on nonessentials.

People are flocking to churches through fear. Americans must have a totally new way of life, become a race of wholly devoted souls, devoted to God and His ways. They must get to a simpler way of life. The standards of America must be lowered, have fewer luxuries. . . . Americans do not have enough belief in God, not enough detachment. They must be more spiritual, disencumber themselves from things, have Bahá'í standards, not American standards. Americans are too materialistic, too mechanized, too attached to family, health, and death. There must be less materialism, less intellectualism, and more spirit. . . . America is the most disturbed nation, politically, on earth. . . . There is too much organization in America and too little spirit.

Joseph Smith was a seer, not a Prophet of God, neither major nor minor Prophet. He had a high standard . . . but the Bahá'ís have a higher standard coupled with God's power that comes direct from God for this age.

We must encourage the marriage of blacks and whites. . . . Bahá'u'lláh was sent to bring about world unity, and world unity is the cornerstone of the Faith of Bahá'u'lláh.

It is not enough to go pioneering; one must start immediately teaching the Faith. . . . For pioneers to leave their posts means the next to arrive will have to go through the difficulties all over again, and it will be twice as difficult for them. . . . As soon as the community is strong enough, one should leave and pioneer elsewhere.

The new race will be wholly devoted souls.

As the hours passed in the presence of Shoghi Effendi, I became more and more aware of his tremendous vision of the Faith and of his one aim to establish good will and peace throughout the world. He was modest about his efficiency, but one could not ignore it. He lovingly encouraged the friends in every country. Rúḥíyyih Khánum said that gossip did not influence the Guardian. No one received any special things for serving the Cause; whether they did it well or poorly, the principle was the same.

Before departing at the end of my pilgrimage, I asked Shoghi Effendi if there were any service I could render him. He said, "Please visit the Bahá'í pioneers on the islands in the Mediterranean and give them my love, cheer them up, and beg them to remain at their posts; for if they leave, those who come to replace them will find it much more difficult. Share with them the spirit of the Holy Places here, particularly that of the Sacred Shrines, and tell them of the latest developments of the Ten Year Crusade."

According to the Guardian's wishes, I traveled among the Mediterranean Islands and visited the pioneers in many places. Wherever Shoghi Effendi asked me to go, I felt secure under his protection and shelter and had no anxiety although I traveled alone through these foreign lands, amid strange surroundings, and spoke only English.

After nine months among the islands I then went, on the Guardian's advice, to serve in Europe—to Palma, Majorca—where I remained for a year, living with the Deleurans (Knights of Bahá'u'lláh) until there were fifteen believers. Next I took up my post in Salzburg, Austria, where, while hospitalized, I was able to teach Editha Wehlere and Fritzi Klap and later Raymond Kralitz, the only three native Austrian believers to come into the Faith in Salzburg during the Ten Year Crusade.

'Abdu'l-Bahá had visited a small group of believers in Vienna, April 18–25, 1913. It was a joyous occasion for the Bahá'ís of Austria, and for those of us who were pioneering there, when the National Spiritual Assembly of

Austria was formed in April 1959, in Vienna, with Hand of the Cause of God John Ferraby presiding.

From Salzburg I attended the funeral of Shoghi Effendi. While waiting to go through Customs at the London Airport, an official there asked me who the large crowd of people were, as they seemed to be friends, and why we had come to London. I explained, and he said, "Never have so many people from so far, from so many countries, passed through the London Airport at one time to pay tribute to one person."

After the death of Shoghi Effendi a new era in the Bahá'í Faith began. The believers all over the world arose with great determination to complete the plans of the Guardian, which would culminate in the Great Jubilee. On April 28, 1963, the first Bahá'í World Congress was held in Royal Albert Hall in London. This Jubilee marked the hundredth anniversary of the Declaration of Bahá'u'lláh's Mission. It was also the climax of the Ten Year Crusade planned by Shoghi Effendi to spread the Message of Bahá'u'lláh all over the world. The goals for the Ten Year Crusade had all been accomplished; the worldwide establishment of Bahá'u'lláh's Faith was achieved.

Royal Albert Hall was beautifully decorated for this wonderful occasion. Over six thousand Bahá'ís came from all parts of the world. Almost every race was represented and large groups from many countries, each group in its own native dress, assembled in one section of the hall. The Hands of the Cause of God who were present told of the great achievements which had been accomplished by the Bahá'í world. The Knights of Bahá'u'lláh were asked to stand and be presented to the audience. Those alert and ardent followers of Bahá'u'lláh, those pioneers who had, with heroic self-sacrifice, set out as champion builders of the World Order of Bahá'u'lláh, were at their "posts" by the date set by Shoghi Effendi, October 1954. They had participated in winning the victories by spreading the Cause through the glorious plan initiated in 1953 by the Guardian who, by his love, his wisdom, his prayers, and his praise, had sustained them.

During the Jubilee, prayers were said in many languages, creating a rare spiritual atmosphere and a bond of love among those present. These were days of great happiness and rejoicing for friends of many years, who had been parted because they were pioneering, and who now met in a most happy reunion. Some of us who had attended Bahá'í conferences and schools in different countries renewed our friendships. It was an especially joyous time for me because my daughter joined me there from California and met the friends with whom I had pioneered in Europe during the Ten Year Crusade.

All of London seemed conscious of an exhilaration in the air wherever the believers gathered; for in hotels, in restaurants, in buses, and on the streets people returned the happy and contagious smiles of the Bahá'ís. The London "Bobbies" near the Hall would smile and say "Alláh-u-Abhá!" The exemplary behavior of the Bahá'ís attracted attention everywhere they went.

On April 30 came the most dramatic moment of the Congress, the moment when the nine members of the first Universal House of Justice were presented to the friends and to the Bahá'í world. The vast audience stood. The believers were filled with indescribable joy, and waves of applause greeted each member as he was introduced to the enraptured assemblage: Charles Wolcott, 'Alí Nakhjavání, H. Borrah Kavelin, Ian Semple, Lutfu'lláh Hakím, David Hofman, Hugh Chance, Amoz Gibson, and Hushmand Fatheázam. There, before our eyes, stood the members of the first Universal House of Justice, "which," 'Abdu'l-Bahá had written, "God hath ordained as the source of all good and freed from all error. . . ."[4] Its function the Master had delineated, and Shoghi Effendi had further stated that it "is to be the exponent and guardian of the Divine Justice which can alone insure the security of, and establish the reign of law and order in, a strangely disordered world."[5] At dinner on the first evening of my pilgrimage in 1954 Shoghi Effendi looked at me and said, "Mrs. Brown, upon the proper functioning of the Local Spiritual Assemblies all over the world depends the Universal House of Justice." Three nights later the Guardian again said this. The evening before I left he repeated the statement once more, very firmly, tapping his forefinger very hard on the table to emphasize the point. The believers in this new era of history are becoming increasingly aware of the unique significance and bounty of The Universal House of Justice.

On the evening of April 30 a large public meeting was held in Royal Albert Hall. The subject was "World Unity With Security." The speakers were Hand of the Cause of God William Sears, Elsie Austin, and Philip Hainsworth. On May 1 Amatu'l-Bahá Rúḥíyyih Khánum was the last speaker of the Congress. Her subject was "Shoghi Effendi, the Sign of God." She told of her life with the Guardian, of his plans for the future to spread the Faith. She spoke of his extreme happiness when the goals were met and said that he constantly praised the believers for their steadfastness and success. Rúḥíyyih Khánum said that Shoghi Effendi prayed daily at the Holy Shrines for all of the friends. She told of his last vacation, when they had visited some of his favorite places, and he had done many of the things he had always enjoyed most. She described how carefully he had selected the furnishings for the Archives Building in Haifa while they were in London. As she shared these precious memories, sadness overcame her, and she wept. Then from behind her came the soft voices of the African believers singing "Alláh-u-Abhá." Absolute stillness pervaded the huge hall as their voices rose to a gentle crescendo, bringing comfort and composure to Rúḥíyyih Khánum; soon she was again her strong, vibrant self. Everyone present felt her sadness and sense of loss, and silently sent their prayerful, loving thoughts to her, and our hearts were filled with overwhelming love for Shoghi Effendi and Rúḥíyyih Khánum.

The World Congress was closed by Hand of the Cause of God Ugo R. Giachery who spoke with loving words of praise, inspiration, and encouragement to the pioneers and believers around the world who had worked so hard to build the World Order of Bahá'u'lláh. Devotions were read, and then the Most Great Jubilee, commemorating "The accession of Bahá'u'lláh to the throne of His sovereignty one hundred years ago in Baghdád," was over.[6]

After the Congress in London I returned to Salzburg, then left on December 23, 1963, for California to avoid another winter in the rigorous climate of Austria. I made plans to return to Salzburg in the spring. However, God evidently had other plans for me, and I returned to San Diego, where I have remained since 1964.[7]

As I gaze out of my window at the blue Pacific, I remember how swiftly the years have passed since 'Abdu'l-Bahá's visit here. Suddenly my thoughts take me to the London Congress in 1963; I am again seated in Royal Albert Hall, surrounded by more than six thousand Bahá'ís from all over the world celebrating the centenary of Bahá'u'lláh's declaration and the election of the first Universal House of Justice. As I think of that vast assemblage of believers, I compare it to the little band of followers in the early days of the Faith in California; I relive the glorious days when the Master was in our midst; I remember His instructions, His appeals, His hopes, and His wishes for this small group of believers; I recall the love and devotion He showered upon us and the wisdom with which He taught us. He gave us the courage and inspiration to meet whatever lay ahead.

Notes

Notes

Preface

1. Shoghi Effendi, *The World Order of Bahá'u'lláh: Selected Letters*, 2d rev. ed. (Wilmette, Ill.: Bahá'í Publishing Trust, 1974), p. 81.
2. Shoghi Effendi used the term "mother teacher of the West" for Lua Getsinger (*God Passes By*, rev. ed. [Wilmette, Ill.: Bahá'í Publishing Trust, 1974], p. 257).—ED.
3. 'Abdu'l-Bahá, *Tablets of Abdul-Baha Abbas*, 3 vols. (New York: Bahai Publishing Society, 1909–1916), III, 714.
4. According to H. M. Balyuzi (*'Abdu'l-Bahá: The Centre of the Covenant of Bahá'u'lláh* [London: George Ronald, 1971], p. 404) and Hussein A. Afnan ("The Death of Mirza Abul-Fazl," *Star of the West*, 14, no. 19 [Mar. 2, 1914], 315) Mírzá Abu'l-Faḍl died on January 21, 1914.—ED.

Part 1: *Early Believers in California*

1. 'Abdu'l-Bahá, *Tablets of Abdul-Baha Abbas*, 3 vols. (New York: Bahai Publishing Society, 1909–1916), I, 70.
2. According to a history of Helen Goodall in *Star of the West* ("A Pioneer at the Golden Gate," 13, no. 8 [Nov. 1922], 203) and an account in the papers of Ella Cooper in the National Bahá'í Archives, Wilmette, Illinois, Helen Goodall and Ella Goodall Cooper first heard about the Bahá'í Faith in 1898 through the efforts of Lua and Edward Getsinger, who had come from the East to spread the Teachings in California, and Phoebe Hearst, who invited Lua to give classes in her home.

One of her students, Helen (Nellie) Hillyer, a young friend of Ella's was attracted to the Faith and told the Goodalls about it. Lua was preparing to leave for the Holy Land with Phoebe Hearst, but Helen and Ella were so interested in the new Faith that they went to New York in search of a Bahá'í teacher and studied there with the Syrian Anṭún Ḥaddád. See also "Ella Goodall Cooper," *The Bahá'í World: A Biennial International Record, Volume XII, 1950–1954,* comp. National Spiritual Assembly of the Bahá'ís of the United States (Wilmette, Ill.: Bahá'í Publishing Trust, 1956), pp. 681–84.

3. Quoted in Marion Yazdi, "Kanichi Yamamoto, 1879–1961," *The Bahá'í World: An International Record, Volume XIII, 1954–1963,* comp. The Universal House of Justice (Haifa: The Universal House of Justice, 1970), p. 31.—ED.

4. National Bahá'í Archives, Wilmette, Illinois; the house style for the transliteration of Persian and Arabic words and for punctuation has been used.

5. Ella Goodall and Nellie Hillyer were invited to join Phoebe Hearst's party, which reached 'Akká for pilgrimage in March 1899. See "Pioneer at the Golden Gate," p. 203, and "Ella Goodall Cooper," *Bahá'í World, Vol. XII,* pp. 681–82.

6. "Ella Goodall Cooper," *Bahá'í World, Vol. XII,* p. 682.

7. Quoted in Helen S. Goodall and Ella Goodall Cooper, *Daily Lessons Received at 'Akká January 1908,* rev. ed. (Wilmette, Ill.: Bahá'í Publishing Trust, 1979), pp. 84–85.—ED.

8. National Bahá'í Archives, Wilmette, Illinois. The house style for the transliteration of Persian and Arabic words and of punctuation has been used. On the original Tablet the seal of 'Abdu'l-Bahá appears on the upper right-hand corner of the first page and means "O my two fellow prisoners."

9. Lua Getsinger was one of the first Bahá'ís in the Western world. See Amine DeMille, "Lua Getsinger—Herald of the Covenant," *Bahá'í News,* no. 489 (Dec. 1971), pp. 2–5.—ED.

10. The correct title is the World's Columbian Exposition.—ED.

11. Georgia Ralston, in her memoirs, pp. 6–7 (National Bahá'í Archives, Wilmette, Illinois), and Juliet Thompson in hers (National Bahá'í Archives, Wilmette, Illinois) indicate that the episode took place in New York.—ED.

12. Quoted in "In Memoriam: Mrs. Lua Moore Getsinger,"

Star of the West, 7, no. 4 (May 17, 1916), 29.

13. Quoted in "The Work in California," *Star of the West*, 2, no. 13 (Nov. 4, 1911), 6.—ED.

14. 'Abdu'l-Bahá, "The Body of Man . . . : Tablet from Abdul-Baha to Shanaz Waite," *Star of the West*, 11, no. 19 (Mar. 2, 1921), 318.—ED.

15. This episode occurred before 'Abdu'l-Bahá visited California.—ED.

16. This incident is described by Juliet Thompson in her diary.—ED.

17. According to "In Memoriam: Mrs. Lua Moore Getsinger," p. 29, Lua met the S̲h̲áh in Paris.—ED.

18. Quoted in ibid.—ED.

19. Ahmad Sohrab, "The Lofty Summit of Unchanging Purpose: Words of Abdul-Baha to Lua Getsinger, Ramleh, Egypt, August 19, 1913, From the Diary of Mirza Ahmad Sohrab," *Star of the West*, 4, no. 12 (Oct. 16, 1913), 208. According to Ahmad Sohrab 'Abdu'l-Bahá gave the instructions to Lua while she was in Ramlih, Egypt.—ED.

20. Phoebe Hearst was born in Franklin County, Missouri, on December 3, 1842.—ED.

21. The trip was organized earlier, as the group arrived in 'Akká in December 1898. The party of fourteen included servants.—ED.

22. Phoebe A. Hearst, "Two Letters of Mrs. Phoebe A. Hearst," in *The Bahá'í World: A Biennial International Record, Volume VII, 1936–1938*, comp. National Spiritual Assembly of the Bahá'ís of the United States and Canada (New York: Bahá'í Publishing Committee, 1939), p. 801.—ED.

23. May Maxwell, *An Early Pilgrimage*, 2d rev. ed. (London: George Ronald, 1969), p. 36.

24. After the pilgrimage May Maxwell returned to Paris, where she established the first Bahá'í community in Europe. See Shoghi Effendi, *God Passes By*, pp. 259–60, and Marion Holley, "May Ellis Maxwell," *The Bahá'í World: A Biennial International Record, Volume VIII, 1938–1940*, comp. National Spiritual Assembly of the Bahá'ís of the United States and Canada (Wilmette, Ill.: Bahá'í Publishing Committee, 1942), p. 634.—ED.

25. Shoghi Effendi, *Messages to America: Selected Letters and Cablegrams Addressed to the Bahá'ís of North America, 1932–1946*

(Wilmette, Ill.: Bahá'í Publishing Committee, 1947), p. 38.

26. Later at least one other black employed by Mrs. Hearst accepted the Faith: Charles Tinsley, who is mentioned on pp. 46–47. Ella Cooper to Horace Holley, Feb. 16, 1946, National Bahá'í Archives, Wilmette, Illinois.

27. The account in H. M. Balyuzi, *'Abdu'l-Bahá: The Centre of the Covenant of Bahá'u'lláh* (London: George Ronald, 1971), p. 72, differs.—ED.

28. Hearst, "Two Letters," p. 801.—ED.

29. Phoebe Hearst was a regent of the University of California.—ED.

30. Phoebe Hearst died on April 13, 1919.—ED.

31. Quoted in Shoghi Effendi, *God Passes By*, p. 257.—ED.

32. *In Galilee* (Chicago: Bahai Publishing Society, 1908); *The Bahá'í Revelation* (New York: Bahá'í Publishing Committee, n.d.).—ED.

33. Quoted in Mirza Ahmad Sohrab, "Abdul-Baha at the Grave of Thornton Chase: Los Angeles, California, October 19, 1912," *Star of the West*, 3, no. 13 (Nov. 4, 1912), 15.—ED.

34. Ibid.—ED.

35. Upon her return to California in 1903 Emogene Hoagg organized, with Helen Goodall and her daugher, the first regular Bahá'í meetings in Oakland. See "Henrietta Emogene Martin Hoagg, 1869–1945," *The Bahá'í World: A Biennial International Record, Volume X, 1944–1946*, comp. National Spiritual Assembly of the Bahá'ís of the United States and Canada (Wilmette, Ill.: Bahá'í Publishing Committee, 1949), p. 521.—ED.

36. Our loving appreciation shall forever go to Shoghi Effendi for adding that magnificent translation to his many other precious gifts to the Bahá'í world: his translations of the Writings of Bahá'u'lláh, the Báb, and 'Abdu'l-Bahá.

37. Bahá'u'lláh, *Gleanings from the Writings of Bahá'u'lláh*, trans. Shoghi Effendi, 2d rev. ed. (Wilmette, Ill.: Bahá'í Publishing Trust, 1976), p. 277.

38. Quoted in Ella Goodall Cooper, "Henrietta Emogene Martin Hoagg, 1869–1945," p. 525.

39. Georgia Ralston, in her memoirs, pp. 3–4, records that she went with Lua Getsinger to Chicago and New York to see 'Abdu'l-Bahá. It was not on her first visit to 'Abdu'l-Bahá that He called her His daughter.—ED.

40. 'Abdu'l-Bahá told Georgia Ralston: " 'The lights are very brilliant and very beautiful, but they are as nothing compared to the lights of heaven. Mortal eyes cannot endure the brilliance of the heavenly lights.' " Ralston memoirs, p. 9.—ED.

41. 'Abdu'l-Bahá asked Fujita to travel with Him to California and afterwards sent for him to come to Haifa. See Balyuzi, *'Abdu'l-Bahá*, pp. 266–67.—ED.

42. The Universal House of Justice cabled news of the passing of Fujita on May 9, 1976.—ED.

43. Goodall and Cooper, *Daily Lessons*, p. 86.

44. According to "Pioneer at the Golden Gate," p. 206, the first contribution from the Occident was made by the Oakland Spiritual Assembly in 1903. The Bahá'í community in Hawaii was farther west than Oakland.—ED.

45. See Shoghi Effendi, *God Passes By*, p. 262.—ED.

46. National Bahá'í Archives, Wilmette, Illinois; the house style for the transliteration of Persian and Arabic words and for punctuation has been used.

47. Ella Bailey was eighty-eight when she died. See Robert L. Gulick, Jr., "Ella M. Bailey," *Bahá'í World, Vol. XII*, pp. 685–88.

Part 2: *'Abdu'l-Bahá in California*

1. Quoted in Ella G. Cooper, "Helen S. Goodall," p. 7, National Bahá'í Archives, Wilmette, Illinois.

2. According to H. M. Balyuzi, *'Abdu'l-Bahá: The Centre of the Covenant of Bahá'u'lláh* (London: George Ronald, 1971), p. 286, and Allan L. Ward, *239 Days: 'Abdu'l-Bahá's Journey in America* (Wilmette, Ill.: Bahá'í Publishing Trust, 1979), p. 165, 'Abdu'l-Bahá arrived in California on October 1, 1912. However, the dates of 'Abdu'l-Bahá's trip between September 1 and October 3, 1912, are subject to further verification.—ED.

3. 'Abdu'l-Bahá, "Abdu'l-Baha's 'Welcome' to California: Address Delivered at the Home of Mrs. Helen S. Goodall, Oakland, California, October 3, 1912," *Star of the West*, 4, no. 11 (Sept. 27, 1913), 190, 194.

4. Ibid., p. 190. *Star of the West* prints this paragraph as the introduction to the talk given in the home of Mrs. Goodall.—ED.

5. Ahmad Sohrab, "Interview Between Abdul-Baha and a

San Francisco Newspaper Reporter: To a Correspondent of *The Examiner*, October 3, 1912. . . . From the Diary of Mirza Ahmad Sohrab," *Star of the West*, 4, no. 12 (Oct. 16, 1913), 207.

6. Mírzá Valíyyu'lláh Khán Varqá reported that Bahá'u'lláh once described "'the Power of the Great Ether'" that is given to certain souls by God and exhorted, "'now look to the Master, for this Power is His.'" Quoted in Lady Blomfield (Sitárih Khánum), *The Chosen Highway* (Wilmette, Ill.: Bahá'í Publishing Trust, 1970), p. 134.

7. Balyuzi, *'Abdu'l-Bahá*, p. 288, reports two thousand; "Abdul Baha, the Bahai Prophet, Speaks at Stanford University," *The Palo Altan*, p. 1, reports "nearly two thousand."—ED.

8. "To the World of Science: Address Delivered by Abdul Baha at Stanford University, Palo Alto, Cal., Oct. 8, 1912, 10:15 A.M.," *Palo Altan*, Nov. 1, 1912, p. 4. The Master's talk, printed in the *Palo Altan*, is published in 'Abdu'l-Bahá, *The Promulgation of Universal Peace: Discourses by Abdul Baha during His Visit to the United States in 1912*, [rev. ed.] in 1 vol. (Wilmette, Ill.: Bahai Publishing Committee, 1943), pp. 342–49.—ED.

9. National Bahá'í Archives, Wilmette, Illinois; the house style for the transliteration of Persian and Arabic words and for punctuation has been used.

10. From notes taken by Frances Allen and published in Frances Orr Allen, "Abdul-Baha in San Francisco, California," *Star of the West*, 3, no. 12 (Oct. 16, 1912), p. 9. The version in "Message to the Church: Address by Abdul Baha, Unitarian Church, Palo Alto, California, (Mr. Clarence Reed, Minister), Tuesday, 8 P.M., October 8, 1912," *Palo Altan*, Nov. 1, 1912, p. 4, differs slightly.

11. Calling George Latimer a "distinguished disciple of 'Abdu'l-Bahá" and a "firm pillar of the American Bahá'í Community," Shoghi Effendi stated that "his outstanding services during the closing years of the Heroic and first epoch of the Formative Ages of the Faith are imperishable." *Citadel of Faith: Messages to America, 1947–1957* (Wilmette, Ill.: Bahá'í Publishing Trust, 1965), p. 166.—ED.

12. "The Visit of Abdul-Baha to Mr. Charles Tinsley: San Francisco, California, October 10, 1912," *Star of the West*, 4, no. 12 (Oct. 16, 1913), 205. Like Robert Turner, Charles Tinsley had

learned of the Faith while he was employed by Phoebe Hearst.—Ed.

13. 'Abdu'l-Bahá, *Promulgation*, p. 364. See also Frances Orr Allen's description of the talk in "Abdul-Baha in San Francisco, California," *Star of the West*, 3, no. 13 (Nov. 4, 1912), 11.

14. National Bahá'í Archives, Wilmette, Illinois.

15. Frances Orr Allen, in "Abdul-Baha in San Francisco, California," *Star of the West*, 3, no. 13 (Nov. 4, 1912), 12, notes that 110 attended.—Ed.

16. 'Abdu'l-Bahá, "Abdul-Baha at the Nineteen-Day Feast: Held October 16, 1912, at the home of Mrs. Helen S. Goodall, Oakland, California," *Star of the West*, 4, no. 12 (Oct. 16, 1913), 203.

17. Ibid.

18. Ibid., p. 209.

19. Frances Orr Allen, "Abdul-Baha in San Francisco, California," *Star of the West*, 3, no. 13 (Nov. 4, 1912), 12. This account suggests the event took place in San Francisco, rather than in Oakland.—Ed.

20. Ibid. The account indicates that 'Abdu'l-Bahá, on the occasion of His visit to the ocean, concluded His talk with these comments.—Ed.

21. 'Abdu'l-Bahá was imprisoned over fifty years.—Ed.

22. Maḥmúd, in his diary, records the date as October 23.—Ed.

23. 'Abdu'l-Bahá, *Tablets of Abdul-Baha Abbas*, 3 vols. (New York: Bahai Publishing Society, 1909–1916), III, 714.

24. Balyuzi, *'Abdu'l-Bahá*, p. 311, dates the final visit to Oakland on October 23; Frances Orr Allen, "Abdul-Baha in San Francisco, California," dates it on October 22. Maḥmúd indicates the final visit took place on October 23, but he includes the reference in his entry for October 22; he has no entry for October 24.—Ed.

25. 'Abdu'l-Bahá, *Promulgation*, p. 317. 'Abdu'l-Bahá made this statement in a talk given in Chicago on September 16.—Ed.

26. 'Abdu'l-Bahá, *Promulgation*, p. 365.

27. Ibid., pp. 365–66.

28. Ibid., pp. 371–72.

Part 3: After 'Abdu'l-Bahá Returned to Haifa

1. 'Abdu'l-Bahá, "Tablet from Abdul-Baha," *Star of the West*, 5, no. 17 (Jan. 19, 1915), 264.
2. 'Abdu'l-Bahá, *Tablets of Abdul-Baha Abbas*, 3 vols. (New York: Bahai Publishing Society, 1909–1916), III, 662–63.
3. Shoghi Effendi, *God Passes By*, rev. ed. (Wilmette, Ill.: Bahá'í Publishing Trust, 1974), pp. 386–87.
4. 'Abdu'l-Bahá, *Tablets of the Divine Plan: Revealed by 'Abdu'l-Bahá to the North American Bahá'ís*, rev. ed. (Wilmette, Ill.: Bahá'í Publishing Trust, 1977), p. 39.
5. Quoted in "The Glad Tidings in Japan," *Star of the West*, 7, no. 5 (June 5, 1916), 35.
6. Many years earlier, in 1931, Mr. Torii had put his longing to make the pilgrimage in these words: "It is my desire some day to visit the Holy Land as 'Abdu'l-Bahá wrote me in his second Tablet dated June 11, 1920, 'whenever the means of travel is secured, thou art permitted to come.'" Tokujiro Torii, "The Bahá'í Movement in Japan," in *The Bahá'í World: A Biennial International Record, Volume IV, 1930–1932*, comp. National Spiritual Assembly of the Bahá'ís of the United States and Canada (New York: Bahá'í Publishing Committee, 1933), p. 493.—Ed.
7. 'Abdu'l-Bahá, *Tablets of the Divine Plan*, p. 81.
8. Ella Cooper sent these words of 'Abdu'l-Bahá to the author in a letter.
9. In 1903, when Bahá'í teachers were needed in California, Kathryn and Alec Frankland moved from Chicago to Fruitvale (now part of Oakland). Later they moved to Los Angeles, to Glendale, and, in 1909, to Mexico City.—'Alí and Marion Yazdí, "Kathryn Frankland: 1872–1963," in *The Bahá'í World: An International Record, Volume XIV, 1963–1968*, comp. The Universal House of Justice (Haifa: The Universal House of Justice, 1974), pp. 338–39.—Ed.
10. See 'Abdu'l-Bahá, *Memorials of the Faithful*, trans. Marzieh Gail (Wilmette, Ill.: Bahá'í Publishing Trust, 1971), pp. 57–59. 'Alí Yazdí passed away on February 18, 1978.—Ed.
11. Charlotte Linfoot passed away on October 30, 1976; Gladys, on October 1, 1977.—Ed.

12. Bahá'u'lláh, in Bahá'u'lláh, The Báb, and 'Abdu'l-Bahá, *Bahá'í Prayers: A Selection of the Prayers Revealed by Bahá'u'lláh, The Báb, and 'Abdu'l-Bahá*, rev. ed. (Wilmette, Ill.: Bahá'í Publishing Trust, 1970), p. 135.

13. Quoted in Shoghi Effendi, *God Passes By*, p. 310.

14. 'Abdu'l-Bahá, *Tablets of the Divine Plan*, p. 79.

15. Shoghi Effendi, *God Passes By*, p. 279.

16. 'Abdu'l-Bahá, *Tablets of Abdul-Baha Abbas*, III, 713.

Part 4: *Coda*

1. 'Abdu'l-Bahá, *Will and Testament of 'Abdu'l-Bahá* (Wilmette, Ill.: Bahá'í Publishing Trust, 1944), pp. 11, 3.

2. See Shoghi Effendi, *God Passes By*, rev. ed. (Wilmette, Ill.: Bahá'í Publishing Trust, 1974), p. 194, and Bahá'u'lláh, *Tablets of Bahá'u'lláh revealed after the Kitáb-i-Aqdas*, comp. Research Department of the Universal House of Justice, trans. Habib Taherzadeh and Committee at Bahá'í World Centre (Haifa: Bahá'í World Centre, 1978), pp. 3–5.—ED.

3. See Shoghi Effendi, *God Passes By*, p. 218.

4. 'Abdu'l-Bahá, *Will and Testament*, p. 14.

5. Shoghi Effendi, *The Advent of Divine Justice*, 3d rev. ed. (Wilmette, Ill.: Bahá'í Publishing Trust, 1969), p. 18.

6. From the printed program of the Jubilee.

7. At the request of the Hand of the Cause of God Ugo Giachery, Mrs. Brown went to San Diego to stay with his ailing wife Angeline while he was in Central America on a teaching trip. On Dr. Giachery's return, Ramona Brown moved to La Jolla, where she passed away on February 23, 1975.

Index

Index

'Abdu'l-Bahá: arrival in America of, 33; arrival in California of, 129 n.2; as Center of the Covenant, 15, 84, 131 n.25; as Exemplar, 53, 63, 81; Day of the Covenant established by, 15; death of, 104; imprisonment of, 17–18, 33, 75; "Mystery of God, the," 85; photograph of, 81; qualities of, 5, **36–38**, 39–40, 43–44, 45–46, 52, 68, 78–79, 84; Shoghi Effendi appointed Guardian by, 105; travels of, 33–34, 35, 38–39, 40, 118. *See also* 'Abdu'l-Bahá, meetings with; 'Abdu'l-Bahá, Tablets from; 'Abdu'l-Bahá, talks and visits of; 'Abdu'l-Bahá, topics discussed by

'Abdu'l-Bahá, meetings with: Allen, Frances, 35–37, 63–64; Allen, Dr. Warren, 35–37, 69–75; Allen, Dr. Woodson, 35–37, 47, 48–49, 69–76; Barr, Marie, 78–81; Bray, Joseph, 66–68; Brown, Ramona Allen, 13–14, **35–37**, 45–46, 59–61, 66–68, 75–76, **78–81**, 83–86, 106–7 passim; Catton, Dr. Joseph, 69–75; Cooper, Ella Goodall, 24, 33, 86, 106–7 passim; Getsinger, Lua, 11–12, 13–14 passim; Goodall, Helen, 24, 33, 47, 63–65, 100 passim; Hearst, Phoebe, 53; Latimer, George, 44; Latimer, Harriett, 44, 87; Latimer, James, 44; Merriman, I. C., 42; Monroe, Anna, 45; Oregon Bahá'ís, 53–58, 61–63; O'Reilly, Cathryn, 58–59, 85; "Peach Tree," 38, 59–61, 66–67, 78–81; Ralston, Georgia, 24–25; Thompson, Juliet, 15; Tinsley, Charles, 46–47; Vent, Betty, 78–81; Washington (state) Bahá'ís, 54–57, 57–59, 61–63, 82–83

'Abdu'l-Bahá, Tablets from: Allen, Frances, 9–10, 103; Bailey, Ella, 29; Cooper, Ella, 8, 91–92; D'Evelyn, Dr. Frederick, 91–92; Getsinger, Lua, 16–17; Goodall, Helen, 7, 30, 91–92; Ralston, Georgia, 91–92; Ralston, William, 91–92; Rogers, Ernest, 42; Storch, Juanita, 91

'Abdu'l-Bahá, talks and visits of: 'Abdu'l-Bahá's San Francisco home, 34–35, 45–46, 49, 53–54, 57–59, 59–61, 64, 77–78, 82–83; Berkeley High School, 40; Berkeley Short Story Club, 40; Chicago, 33, 128 n.39, 131 n.25; First Congregational Church, Oakland, 40–41; Goodall home, 38–39, 50–51, 54–57, 63, 78–81, 83–85; Hacienda, 21, 53; Hotel Sacramento, 87–88; Japanese YMCA, 41; New York, 15,

137

'Abdu'l-Bahá, talks and visits of (*continued*)
126 n.11; Oakland School for the Blind, 40; Peace Society, 40; Sacramento, 85–88, 106–7; San Francisco, 25, 34, 129 n.2; *San Francisco Examiner*, 40; Stanford University, 41, 80, 130 n.7, 130 n.8; Temple Emmanu-El ("Fundamental Unity of Religious Thought"), 49; Theosophical Society, 40; Unitarian Church, Palo Alto ("Reality of Divinity"), 42, 130 n.10

'Abdu'l-Bahá, topics discussed by: Alexander, Agnes, 93; Allen, Dr. Woodson, 99; Báb, The, 7, 15; Bahá'u'lláh, 7, 35, 38, 49, 65, 66–67, 84, 86; Bailey, Ella, 10, 30; California, 61–62, 87–88, 105–6; capacity, 64, 80, 91; Chase, Thornton, 21–23; children, 50–52, 77–78; confirmations, 59–60, 79–80, 87, 92, 97–98; Cooper, Ella, 8, 97; Covenant of Bahá'u'lláh, 15, 84; Day of the Covenant, 15; difficulties, 9, 16, 29, 46–47; Dreyfus, Hippolyte, 97; Dreyfus-Barney, Laura, 97; education, 50–51, 58, 83; feasts, Bahá'í, 30, 47, 54; firmness, 16, 61, 65, 68, 80; Frankland, Kathryn, 97–98; "gardens of God," 50–52, 59–60; Getsinger, Lua, 16, 17; Goodall, Helen, 7, 8, 9–10, 54, 97; happiness, 53–54; healing and health, 48–49, 69–76; Hearst, Phoebe, 19; intuition, 14; International Bahá'í Conference, 1915, 91–92; Japanese Bahá'ís, 87; Jesus and His disciples, 49, 80, 86; love, 45, 47, 55, 62; meetings, 34–35, 39, 54, 55, 57, 63, 64–65; Muḥammad, 49; music, 63; oneness of mankind, 10, 40, 50, 57–58, 98; peace, 40, 50, 87, 92, 97; pilgrimage, 18; prayer, 42, 72–73, 74, 98; pure hearts, 33; Ralston, Georgia, 25, 97; religious unity, 49–50; Resurrection, 7; Root, Martha, 93; San Diego, 12–13; steadfastness, 29, 61, 68, 80, 83; teaching, 16, **59–61**, 63, **66–67**, 78, **79–80**, 81, 85, 86, 98; Tinsley, Charles, 47–48; travels to America, 35, 38–39, 40; unity, 57–58, 61–62; Universal House of Justice, The, 120; Yamamoto, Kanichi, 5

Abu'l-Faḍl, Mírzá, xx, 16, 17, 23, 125 n.4

Administrative Order, 28, 105, 115

Alexander, Agnes, 93–96; becomes Bahá'í, 94–95; death of, 96; pioneering of, 93; qualities of, 96; titles of, 93

Ainu, 95

Ali-Kuli Khan, xx, 10

Allen, Frances Orr: becomes Bahá'í, 4–5; meetings in home of, 10, 64; meetings of, with 'Abdu'l-Bahá, 35–37, 63–64; message to, from 'Abdu'l-Bahá, 99; Tablets to, 9–10, 103

Allen, Dr. Warren, 4, 35–37, 69–75, 76–77

Allen, Dr. Woodson, 9; death of, 76, 99; meetings of, with 'Abdu'l-Bahá, 35–37, 47, 48–49, 69–76

Amatu'l-Bahá Rúḥíyyih Khánum. See Rúḥíyyih Khánum, Amatu'l-Bahá

Anderson, Mrs., 6

Apperson, Ann, 4, 17

Archives Building, 121

Austin, Elsie, 121

Austria, National Spiritual Assembly of, 118–19

Báb, The, 7, 15

Babcock, O. M., 19

Bahá'í Peace Program, The, 88

Bahá'í Revelation, The, 21
Bahá'í World Congress, 1963, 119–22
Bahá'u'lláh: Covenant of, 15, 84, 115; Declaration of, 84, 119; imprisonment and exile of, 5, 65, 66–67, 84; proof of, 67; suffering of, 5, 49, 65, 84; Tablets of, 66, 115. *See also* 'Abdu'l-Bahá, topics discussed by: Bahá'u'lláh
Bailey, Mrs. Ella, 10, 29–30; death of, 10, 30, 129 n.47; "first American martyr in Africa," 29; pioneering of, 29–30; qualities of, 29–30; Tablet to, 29; teaching activities of, 29–30
Baldwin, Katherine, 102
Barr, Marie, 78
Berkeley High School, 40
Berkeley, Local Spiritual Assembly of, 30, 100
Berkeley Short Story Club, 40
Berkeley Women's City Club, 30
Bolles, May. *See* Maxwell, May Bolles
Bosch, John, 96–97
Bosch, Louise, 96–97
Bradford, I[saiah] H., 19
Bray, Allen, 66
Bray, Barbara. *See* West, Barbara Bray
Bray, Joseph Grandin, 14, 65–68
Brittingham, Isabella, 10, 42
Brown, Arthur M., 21, 111
Brown, Ramona Allen: 'Abdu'l-Bahá's impact on, 3, **35–38**, 43–44, 61, 68, 84, 106–7, 122; at Bahá'í World Congress, 1963, 119–22; becomes Bahá'í, xv, 4–6; birth of, xv; death of, xv, 133 n.7; death of 'Abdu'l-Bahá and, 104–5; marriages, 21, 68; meetings in home of, 68, 111; meetings of, with 'Abdu'l-Bahá, 13–14, 35–37, 45–46, 59–61, 66–68, 75–76, 78–81, 83–86, 106–7 passim; "Peach Tree" and, 26–27, 59–61, 66–67, 78–81; pilgrimage of, 1954, xv, 68, 111–14; pioneering of, xvi, 118; teaching activities of, xvi, 111, 118; visits to pioneers by, xvi, 118

California, early Bahá'ís of: Administrative Order and, 28, 105; books available to, 6–7, 11, 28; children's classes of, 98; feasts of, 6, 27–28, 30, 54–57; qualities of, xxi, 3–4, 7–8; state conventions of, 24; unity of, 7–8, 30, 45
California, meetings on battleship, 12
Catton, Dr. Joseph, 69–75
Chance, Hugh, 120
Chase, Thornton, 10, 21–23; books written by, 21; death of, 21; eulogy of, by 'Abdu'l-Bahá, 21–23; "first American believer," 21; pilgrimage of, 21; qualities of, 21, 22–23; teaching activities of, 21, 23
Chicago, 33, 128 n.39, 131 n.25
Children, 50–52, 77–78, 98
Chula Vista, California, 100
"City of the Covenant," 15
Clark, E. H., 20
Collins, Amelia, 95, 112
Cooper, Dr. Charles Minor, 8, 9, 102
Cooper, Ella Goodall, 4, 8–9, 25–27, 101–3; becomes Bahá'í, 4, 125–26 n.2; death of, 103; marriage of, 8–9; meetings of, with 'Abdu'l-Bahá, 24, 86, 106–7; "Mother Peach," 26–27; pilgrimage of, 1898–99, 8, 17, 126 n.5; pilgrimage of, 1908, 25; pilgrimage of, 1920, 97; qualities of, 4, 8, 26, 101–3; Tablet to, 8; teaching activities of, 4, 10, 21, 26–27, 101–2, 111
Covenant of Bahá'u'lláh, 18, 84, 115

INDEX 139

Daily Lessons Received at 'Akká, 25–26
Dawn-Breakers, The, 24, 128 n.36
Day of the Covenant, 15
de Herrera y Puerto, Esperanza, 12
Deleuran, [Jean], 118
Deleuran, [Tove], 118
D'Evelyn, Dr. F[rederick] W., 91–92
Dixon, Mrs., 94–95
Dreyfus, [Hippolyte], 97
Dreyfus[-Barney, Laura], 97
Dunn, Clara, 10
Dunn, Hyde, 10

Education, 50–51, 58, 83
Eggleston, Lou, 103
Elijah, 115
Elston, Alan, 113
Elston, Mary, 113

Faríd, Dr. [Amínulláh], 72, 74
Fatheázam, Hushmand, 120
Feasts, 6, 27–28, 30, 54–57
Ferraby, John, 95, 119
First Congregational Church, Oakland, 40–41
First Western Conference, 101
Ford, Mary Hanford, 10
Frankland, Alec, 98, 100, 132 n.9
Frankland, Kathryn, 25, 97–100; children's classes with, 98; death of, 100; meetings in home of, 98, 132 n.9; pilgrimage of, 1920, 97, 99; qualities of, 98, 99
Fujita, Saichiro, 25, 129 n.41, 129 n.42
"Fundamental Unity of Religious Thought, The," 49–50

Gail, Marzieh, 111
Getsinger, Edward, 11–12, 16, 17, 125 n.2
Getsinger, Lua, 10–17; becomes Bahá'í, 10, 126 n.9; birth of, 10; death of, 17; "Herald of the Covenant," 15; instructions to, from 'Abdu'l-Bahá, 10, 11, 12, 16, 127 n.19; meetings of, with 'Abdu'l-Bahá, 10, 11–12, 13–14, 15, 16, 128 n.39; meeting of, with Sháh of Persia, 15–16, 127 n.17; "Mother Teacher of the West," xx, 125 n.2; qualities of, 11, 14, 16, 19; pilgrimage of, 1898–99, 11–12, 17–18; Tablets to, 16–17; teaching activities of, 10, 11, 12, 13, 15, 16, 19, 23, 24, 125 n.2
Geyserville School, 97, 100
Giachery, Ugo, 95, 121
Gibson, Amoz, 120
Gleanings from the Writings of Bahá'u'lláh, 24
Global Crusade, 115
God Passes By, 106
Goodall, Arthur, 9, 102
Goodall, Ella. See Cooper, Ella Goodall
Goodall, Helen: 'Abdu'l-Bahá in home of, 38–39, 50–51, 54–57, 63, 78–81, 83–85; becomes Bahá'í, 4, 125–26 n.2; death of, 100; feasts in home of, 27–28, 30, 54–57; meetings in home of, 4, 5, 9–10, 26, 128 n.35; pilgrimage of, 1908, 25; pilgrimage of, 1920, 97, 100; qualities of, 4, 7, 8, 26, 97; Shoghi Effendi's praise of, 100; "Spiritual Mother of the Oakland Community," 8; Tablets to, 6, 7, 30, 91–92; teaching activities of, 10, 26
Great Jubilee, 119–22
Greatest Holy Leaf, 18, 99
Greatest Name, 27, 28, 71, 85, 99, 107
Gulick, Bahia, 30, 111
Gulick, Robert, 30

Hacienda, La, 19, 20, 21, 23, 53
Haddád, Antún, 4, 126 n.2
Hainsworth, Philip, 121
Hakím, Lutfu'lláh, 120

Hands of the Cause of God, 67, 119. *See also* Alexander, Agnes; Collins, Amelia; Dunn, Clara; Ferraby, John; Giachery, Ugo; Ioas, Leroy; Khadem, Zikr'u'lláh; Rúḥíyyih Khánum, Amatu'l-Bahá; Sears, William; True, Corinne
Hatch, Willard, 10
Healing and health, 48–49, 69–76
Hearst, George F., 17, 19
Hearst, Phoebe Apperson, 4, 17–21; 'Abdu'l-Bahá visits home of, 21, 53; birth of, 17, 127 n.20; death of, 20, 21, 128 n.30; deepens with Lua Getsinger, 19; meetings in home of, 19, 23, 125 n.2; "Mother of the Faithful," 19; pilgrimage of, 1898-99, 8, 17–18, 126 n.5, 127 n.21; qualities of, 19, 20, 21
Hearst, William Randolph, 20
Herron, Louise, 19
Hidden Words of Bahá'u'lláh, The, 6, 28
Hillyer, Nellie, 17, 126 n.2, 126 n.5
Hoagg, Emogene, 23–24; becomes Bahá'í, 23; birth of, 23; death of, 24; pilgrimage of, 1900, 23, 128 n.35; teaching activities of, 23, 24, 128 n.35
Hofman, David, 120
Honolulu, Hawaii, 96, 102
Hotel Sacramento, 87–88
House of Worship, Wilmette, 27, 30, 100, 111, 129 n.44

In Galilee, 21
International Bahá'í Conference, 1915, 91–92
International Conference in Stockholm, 1953, 111
Ioas, Leroy, 100

Japan, 93–94, 95
Japanese Bahá'ís in Oregon, 87
Japanese YMCA, 41

Jesus, 6, 49, 80, 86
Jordan, David Starr, 41, 42

Kanno, Takeshi, 64
Kavelin, H. Borrah, 120
Keeling, Henry, 101
Khadem, Zikr'u'lláh, 113
Khan, Madame, 55
Klap, Fritzi, 118
Knights of Bahá'u'lláh, 119
Kralitz, Raymond, 118
Kyoto, Japan, 94, 96

La Jolla, California, 12
Lane, Agnes, 19
Latimer, George, 44, 103, 130 n.11
Latimer, Harriett (Ruhaniyyih), 44–45, 87
Latimer, James, 44
Leland Stanford Junior University. *See* Stanford University
Lesser Peace, 115
Linfoot, Annie, 100–101
Linfoot, Charlotte, 100–101, 132 n.11
Linfoot, Gladys, 100–101, 132 n.11
Linfoot, John, 100–101
Linfoot, William, 100–101
Little, Marion, 102
Love, 45, 47, 55, 62 passim

Mack, Mr., 12
Marie, Queen of Rumania, 93
Mathews, Loulie, 111
Matteson, Berdette, 55–56
Matteson, Eleanor, 56
Matteson, Lorne, 56
Matteson, John W., 55–56
Maxwell, Mary. *See* Rúḥíyyih Khánum, Amatu'l-Bahá
Maxwell, May Bolles, 18; becomes Bahá'í, 18; death of, 18; "Mother Teacher of Latin People," 18; pilgrimage of, 1898-99, 17–18, 127 n.24; Shoghi Effendi's tribute to, 18; teaching activities of, 18, 127 n.24

Meetings, 34–35, 39, 55, 57, 63, 64–65
Memorials of the Faithful, 98
Merriman, I. C., 42
Mexico City, Mexico, 132 n.9
Meyer, Rabbi Martin A., 49
Monroe, Anna, 5, 45
Montezuma Mountain School for Boys, 41
Most Great Jubilee, 119–22
Most Great Peace, 115
Muḥammad, 49
Muḥammad-ʿAlí Ṣabbáq of Yazd, 98–99

Nakhjavání, ʿAlí, 120
National Congress of Parents and Teachers, 20
National Spiritual Assembly, 44, 101
Navváb, 84
New York, 15, 126 n.11

Oakland, California, 3
Oakland, Local Spiritual Assembly of, 100
Oakland School for the Blind, 40
Oregon Baháʾís, 53–59, 61–63, 87
O'Reilly, Cathryn, 58–59, 85

Palo Alto, California, 12, 42
Panama-Pacific International Exposition, 1915, 20, 92
Pan American International Exposition, 1915, 101
Peace, 40, 50, 87, 92, 97
Peace Society, 40
"Peach Tree," 26–27, 38, 59–61, 66–67, 78–81
Phoebe Apperson Hearst Memorial Association, 20
Pinson, Josephine, 24
Point Loma, California, 12
'Power of the Great Ether,' 41, 130 n.6
Prefectural School for the Blind, 94

Ralston, Georgia Grayson, 24–25; becomes Baháʾí, 24; "daughter" of ʿAbduʾl-Bahá, 24–25; meeting of, with ʿAbduʾl-Bahá, 24–25, 128 n.39, 129 n.40; pilgrimage of, 1920, 25, 97; qualities of, 24–25; Tablet to, 91–92
Ralston, William C., 24, 91–92
Reagan, Ronald, 20
"Reality of Divinity," 42
Reed, Rev. Clarence, 42
Revell, Jessie, 111
Rexford, Orcella, 100
Riverside, California, 100
Robinson, Alice, 55
Robinson, Mr., 55
Rogers, Dr. Ernest, 41–42
Root, Martha, 10, 93; death of, 93; Marie, Queen of Rumania, and, 93; Shoghi Effendi's praise of, 93; teaching activities of, 93
Ruhaniyyih. *See* Latimer, Harriett
Rúḥíyyih Khánum, Amatuʾl-Bahá (Mary Maxwell), 18, 112, 114, 121

Sacramento, California, 85–88, 106–7
Sala, 113
Salzburg, Austria, 100, 118
San Diego, Prayer for 12–13
San Diego Women's City Club, 12, 101
San Francisco, Local Spiritual Assembly of, 101
San Francisco Examiner, 40
San Francisco Memorial Opera House, 88
Sears, William, xix, 121
Semple, Ian, 120
Seven Year Plans, 106
Sháh of Persia, 15–16, 127 n.17
Shoghi Effendi: appointment of, as Guardian, 105; as "priceless pearl," 112; death of, 105, 119; funeral of, 119; qualities of,

112–13, 118; translations by, 24, 67, 128 n.36. *See also* Shoghi Effendi, topics discussed by
Shoghi Effendi, topics discussed by: 'Abdu'l-Bahá, 106; Bahá'í life, 114, 117; Bahá'u'lláh, 114, 115; capacity, 114; Covenant of Bahá'u'lláh, 115; destruction in America, 116–17; early American Bahá'ís, xix; future temples and Houses of Justice, 114; Getsinger, Lua, 125 n.2; Goodall, Helen, 100; House of Worship, Wilmette, 27; intellectualism, 117; intermarriage, 117; Lesser Peace, 115; materialism, 117; Most Great Peace, 115; Maxwell, May, 18; pioneering, 115–16, 117, 118; Root, Martha, 93; service,114; Smith, Joseph, 117; Tablet of Carmel, 115; teaching, 115, 117; Universal House of Justice, The, 120–21; United States of the World, 115; Will and Testament, 115
"Shoghi Effendi: the Sign of God," 121
Smith, Joseph, 117
Stanford University, 41, 80, 130 n.7, 130 n.8
Stockholm International Conference, 1953, 111
Storch, Juanita, 91
Straun, Bijou, xx
Sulaymáníyyih, 84

Tablet of Carmel, 115
Tablet of the Branch, 15, 127 n.15
Tablets of 'Abdu'l-Bahá, 13, 81, 106
Tablets of the Divine Plan, 92–93, 96, 97, 105–6
Tahiti, 97
Teaching, 24, 59–61, 66–67, 79–81, 115. *See also* 'Abdu'l-Bahá, topics discussed by: teaching
Temple Emmanu-El, 49

Ten Year Crusade, 30, 106, 118, 119, 120
Theosophical Society, 40
Thompson, Juliet, 15
"Three Conditions of Existence, The," 24
Tijuana, Mexico, 12
Tinsley, Charles, 46–47, 128 n.26
Tobey, Mark, 111
Torii, Tokujiro, 94, 132 n.6
True, Corinne, 25
Truman, Harry S., 88
Turner, Robert, 18, 128 n.27

Unitarian Church, Palo Alto, 42, 130 n.10
United Nations Charter, 88
Unity. *See* 'Abdu'l-Bahá, topics discussed by: oneness of mankind, religious unity, unity
Universal House of Justice, The, 120
Universal Peace, 40, 50, 87, 92, 97
University of California, Berkeley, 20

Vent, Betty, 78
Vienna, 118–19
Visitation Tablet, 104

Washington (state) Bahá'ís, 54–59, 61–63, 82–83
Wehlere, Editha, 118
West, Barbara Bray, 66, 111
West, "Bobbin," 111
West, David Lee, 67
West, Richard Allen, 67
Whitney, Helen, 103
Will and Testament of 'Abdu'l-Bahá, 105, 115
Wilson, Stitt, 40
Wolcott, Charles, 120
World Center of the Faith, 115
World Congress, Chicago, 1893, 10, 126 n.10
World Congress. *See* Bahá'í World Congress

INDEX 143

World Order of Bahá'u'lláh,The, xix
"World Unity with Security," 121
World's Columbian Exposition, 10, 126 n.10

Yamamoto, Kanichi, 5, 26
Yazdí, 'Alí, 98–99
Yazdí, Marion, 99
Young Turk Revolution, 33